INSIGHT COMPACT GUIDE

Ita Lakes

GW00362753

GREAT LITTLE GUIDES

Compact Guide: Italian Lakes is the ideal quick-reference guide to this classic destination. It tells you everything you need to know about the region's attractions, from medieval towns and their castles to magnificent Renaissance villas and their gardens, from the relative relaxation of the lakeshore to drives and hiking trails through the mountains.

This is one of 120 Compact Guides, which combine the interests and enthusiasms of two of the world's best known information providers: Insight Guides, whose titles have set the standard for visual travel guides since 1970, and Discovery Channel, the world's premier source of nonfiction television programming.

Star Attractions

An instant reference to some of the Italian Lakes' most popular tourist attractions to help you on your way.

Ascona cloister p17

Isola Bella, Maggiore p21

Lake Lugano p28

Lugano sculpture p 29

Como Cathedral p36

Bellagio p44

Malcesine p 58

Sirmione castle p63

Gardone Riviera p 68

Madonna di Monte Castello p69

Verona p74

Italian Lakes

Introduction

Places

Culture

Leisure

Practical Information

Italian Lakes – A Region for all Tastes

Opposite: Isola di Garda

Views wherever you look

The Northern Italian Lakes are one of the most fascinating regions of Italy, and also one of the most popular with tourists. Their waters ensure that winters stay pleasantly mild, and summers pleasantly cool. Their shores are lined with elegant villas surrounded by delightful parks and gardens. The region is also justly famed for its magnificent views and vistas, and a drive through this part of Italy is often a challenge to intrepid motorists as well as being an unforgettable visual treat.

The Northern Italian Lakes – Maggiore, Como, Lugano, Garda and the many smaller ones – are surrounded by the Swiss Ticino and the Italian regions of Lombardy and Piedmont, all of them areas steeped in history and with no end of superb cultural sights to visit, ranging from pre-historic remains and Roman ruins to finely-crafted Lombard Romanesque churches and magnificent Renaissance architecture. The lakes region, where Italy meets the Alps and northern Europe, has always been of enormous strategic importance historically, and the beautiful landscape is enhanced still further by dozens of castles and fortresses, including those built by Verona's most famous medieval family, the Scaligeri, along the shores of Lake Garda. Verona has almost as many as Rome itself, while Bergamo owes its architectural beauty and harmony to the many years of Venetian rule there. These cities and also many of the smaller towns contain first-class art galleries, with priceless paintings by artists such as Titian, Raphael, Tintoretto and Mantegna.

5

Villa d'Este at Cernobbio

Grotte di Catullo on Lake Garda

In the days before mass tourism, Lake Como in particular was a holiday retreat for British connoisseurs of good taste, including writers. Wordsworth lived there in 1790, Byron and Shelley were both regular visitors, and DH Lawrence made it his home from 1925 to 1927. Visitors today can not only bask in the extraordinary cultural landscape and scenery that the region possesses, but also enjoy many activities associated with a modern tourist infrastructure, such as windsurfing, waterskiing or golf. Hikers and climbers can take to the mountains, while those in search of relaxation can sunbathe on the shore or enjoy the spectacular views from the deck of a steamer. In addition to all this, the region is justly famed for its food and also its wines, many of which bear familiar names such as *Bardolino*, *Valpolicella* and *Soave*.

These are just a few of the reasons why the Italian Lakes have exerted such an irresistible attraction on tourists for so many years now. And last but not least of course, there are the Italians themselves – happy, spontaneous and friendly. Welcome to one of the most beautiful and exciting parts of Italy.

Position and landscape

The lakes lie in Upper Italy between the Lombardy Plain and the high Alps. Each lake has its own individual character and shape: they are all long and thin (known as ribbon lakes), but Maggiore, the second largest lake (66km/41 miles long), has a kink in it like the hind leg of a horse, Lugano and Como resemble upside down 'Y's, while Garda, the largest lake (51km/33 miles long), has a bulbous bottom, like a retort. All these shapes are the result of complex local geology and the process of glaciation that took place during the Ice Age (*see below*). While the southern end of Lake Garda extends into the plain, Lake Como is surrounded by mountains. Even though it is only the third-largest lake in Upper Italy (50km/32 miles long), Como is actually the deepest inland lake in Europe (410m/1,350ft).

Though not as high as the central Alps, the mountains surrounding the lakes provide an impressive backdrop. The summit of Monte Legnone (2,609m/8,560ft) towers more than 2,400m (7,900ft) over the surface of Lake Como – at a horizontal distance of only 6km (4 miles) from the shore. It is the highest summit in the region described, but there are other impressive and beautiful massifs around Como, notably the limestone Grigna (2,409m/7,903ft). The Ticino Alps around Maggiore to the west, though not quite so high, still have some fine peaks, including the Gridone (2,188m/ 7,178ft) and Monte Zeda (2,156m/ 7,070ft). Away to the east, Lake Garda is separated from the Adige valley by the narrow ridge of Monte Baldo which rises almost 2,000m (6,500ft) above the lake.

Lake Maggiore is drained by the Ticino river, Lake Como by the Adda, Lake Garda by the Mincio. All of them are tributaries of the Po, which flows into the Adriatic.

Val Cannobina

Diving into Lake Garda

Geology

Some 350 million years ago, much of present day Upper Italy was covered by a tropical sea. As the marine life died it was deposited on the sea bed, where it consolidated in layers, until around 60 million years ago when massive movements of the earth's crust resulted in the creation of the Alps. Around 2 million years ago, during the Pleistocene period, the rivers that flowed into the Po from the Apennines and the Alps brought a great deal of alluvial silt with them; this was deposited on the Plain of Lombardy and is the reason why the whole area has remained so fertile to this day.

Prior to the last Ice Age, there were no lakes in the region, but simply large valleys. During this Ice Age the rivers became powerful glaciers, and massive basins were gouged out of the rock. The level of the bottom of these

Isola di Garda

ew basins was considerably lower than that of the exit
o the valleys, so after the glaciers retreated and the val-
eys filled up with water, the resultant lakes were extremely
deep, their bottoms lying well below sea level. Additional
depth was created by the morraine debris the glaciers left
behind as they retreated. The deepest part of Lake Garda,
for instance, is 346m (1,135ft), with the moraine thickness
of 149m (488ft) making up almost half of that. The glaciers left behind not only lakes but also highly complex
drainage patterns, seen, for example in the two arms of
Lake Como, one of which has no outflow at all, and in
Lake Orta to the west of Lake Maggiore, which drains out
to the north.

The mountains defining the lakes are not of uniform
structure. To the north of Lake Garda, they are formed
of a specialised form of limestone known as Dolomite. Between Garda and Como, the prevalent rock is granite,
whose resistance to erosion explains the fact that no large
lake has been formed in that area. Around Como and Maggiore, it's largely limestone again, though intrusions of
crystalline rock (schists and gneiss) become more pro-
nounced the further west you go.

Climate and when to go

The Mediterranean type climate of the Italian lakes is
one of the main reasons tourists are so attracted to the area.
Despite their proximity to the Alps and central European
location, the lakes are so large that they actually distort the
local climate, making winters warmer than is usual for this
latitude and summers slightly cooler. However, because
of the mountain environment the weather on Lakes Maggiore, Como and particularly Garda isn't all that pre-
dictable: in spring and autumn, be prepared for sudden
cloudbursts (most likely to occur in May and September).

*Como: Villa dell'Olmo and
Tempio Voltano*

Tremezzo: Villa Carlotta gardens

Formal gardens in Verona

Even in January, snowfalls are very rare at lake level and by the beginning of April the sun is as warm as it is elsewhere in Europe in mid-May. In the summer a fresh breeze keeps the temperatures pleasant even when there isn't a cloud in the sky. The relatively steady winds blowing up and down the lakes make them a paradise for wind surfers and sailors.

The water is also a very pleasant 25°C (77°F) during July and August. Many like to visit the lakes in the spring time, when there is a profusion of blossom and the villas with their parks and gardens are utterly magnificent. Swimmers tend to favour early summer through to September as a good time for a holiday. Autumn is ideal for long hikes and serene contemplation of (relatively) tourist free scenery, and the service is a lot better in the restaurants because the staff have more time. Winter is quiet and many places close down for the season.

Summer grazing

Flora and fauna

In January, when everything north of the Alps is usually under a blanket of snow, rose, jasmine and laurels are already blooming in Northern Italy. In February, the mimosa and forsythia herald the spring with their intense yellow blossom, and in March the camellias, magnolias, oleander, gorse and peach-trees all burst into blossom. The whole scene is quite Mediterranean, and it's hard to believe that such splendour actually exists miles inland. The vegetation is as varied as the local fauna. Reptiles are common, especially lizards and the odd snake. A lot of animals are active at night, such as wild pigs, foxes and bats. All lakes have an abundance of fish, including trout, eel, carp and whitefish, though until urgent remedial action was recently taken by the authorities, stocks were under serious threat from water pollution.

anguage

n omm al gheva a düü fiö ('A man had two sons') could
 the opening of any local fairytale, and anyone who's
 st done a course in Italian will be annoyed to discover
 at he doesn't understand a word. The strange language
 Lombardian. Never fear, however: only a few small
 mmunities high in the mountains continue to commu-
cate in it. The language of Dante – which marked the be-
 nning of Italian literature – was Tuscan, and over the
 nturies Lombardian was gradually squeezed out by Tus-
 n Italian as the favoured dialect.

Friendly locals

conomy

 ombardy is considered the 'powerhouse of Italy', and so
 's no wonder that the towns along the edge of the Alps
 'arese, Como, Lecco) are largely industrial. The most
 viously industrial areas are in the Brianza and around
 omo; the latter, famous as the *città della seta* (city of
 lk), has diversified a lot over the past few decades and
 come as industrial as Varese. Ironworking has taken over
 om silk as the main industry around Lake Como.

As far as agriculture is concerned, the higher plains
 e suited to the cultivation of cereals, including maize
 or polenta), green vegetables, fruit trees and mulber-
 es (for silk cocoons). The hilly zone has fruit and chest-
 it trees, and the soil around the lakes is especially suitable
 r olive trees and limes. Vines grow to an altitude of 850m
 ,400ft), and on the Alpine meadows there is excellent
 azing for both cattle (half of which are milk produc-
 g) and sheep (bred for wool as well as meat).

Rural lifestyles

9

A vital part of economy is tourism. Lake Garda alone
 s more than 5 million foreign visitors a year. The sheer
 ealth of cultural sights combined with the astonishing
 riety of activities on offer acts as an irresistible mag-
 t to tourists from all over the world; one reason why
 ummer accommodation beside any of the lakes these days
 ould be booked at least six months in advance.

Vineyards in Custoza

However, not all the inhabitants of the region have
 ined from its prosperity. Whenever you travel a short
 stance inland from the roads around these lakes it be-
 mes clear just how deserted many of the villages in the
 ral areas have become. The steep peaks and deep ravines,
 picturesque for the traveller, are often part of a never-
 ding struggle for survival for the poor people living in
 gions like the Grigna. Young people have been leav-
 g for the towns and big cities to set up a new life for them-
 lves in safer and more comfortable surroundings. Only
 cently has there been a movement among young peo-
 e *away* from the smog and hectic lifestyle and back to
 e peace of the countryside – and it is growing steadily
 ore popular.

Historical Highlights

9,000BC Settlers arrive in the fertile Po Plain as the ice sheets withdraw.

7th century BC The Celts head southwards, and their settlements later develop into some of Northern Italy's finest cities, including Milan, Como and Bergamo. The Celts trade busily with the Etruscans, who cross the Apennines as far as Mantua.

4th century BC The Gauls cross the Alps, sacking Rome in 390BC.

3rd century BC The Romans move northwards to drive out the Gauls and bring the whole of northern Italy under their control.

191BC The region becomes the Roman province of Gallia Cisalpina. The capital is Mediolanum (Milan), vital as a strategic crossroads between territories to the east, west and south, as well as a springboard for future expansion to the north. The Romans lay the foundations of the industrial triangle between Milan, Genoa and Turin.

2nd century BC Bergamo and Como both become Roman colonies.

89BC Verona becomes a Roman colony.

59–49BC Under the governorship of Caesar, Verona, too, becomes a strategically important crossroads and develops into a major administrative and commercial centre.

AD286 Diocletian assigns Milan as residence and main administrative centre to his emperor-colleague, Maximian.

AD313 Under the Edict of Milan, Constantine the Great grants freedom of worship to Christians.

4th century AD The Upper Italian lake area becomes a transit region for French and English pilgrims on their way to Rome.

AD330 Constantine moves the capital of the Empire to Byzantium.

5th century Following the division of the Empire into two halves in 393, the western part becomes weakened and vulnerable to attacks by warlike tribes of central Europe.

403 Verona is besieged by the Visigoths under Alaric.

452 The forces of Attila the Hun lay waste Verona and the Po Plain.

476 End of the western Empire. The German leader Odoacer conquers northern Italy.

568 The Lombards, a Teutonic tribe, invade northern Italy. Within a year they have conquered all the cities north of the River Po, and soon assume control of the lakes region, and call it Lombardy. In the latter part of the 7th century, the Lombards are converted to Christianity by Theodolinda, daughter of a Bavarian duke.

774 After the invasion of the papal territories by the Lombard kings, Charlemagne is summoned by the pope. He destroys the Lombard kingdom and creates a Frankish state in northern Italy.

9th–10th centuries Bishops of cities such as Bergamo and Como obtain a succession of sovereign privileges, exercising civil as well as ecclesiastical rule over entire districts.

962 Otto the Great retakes Italy, heralding the start of almost 200 years of attempted German domination in the area.

11th–16th centuries The period of the Italian city states. In northern Italy, Milan, Bergamo and Verona all begin to thrive from the burgeoning overland trade with the Orient. At first power is in the hands of the merchants, but later belongs to just a few local families (*Signori*). Verona and Garda it is the della Scalas (Scaligeri), in Milan the Visconti.

11th–12th centuries Having declared itself an autonomous commune, in the ensuing struggle for primacy among the cities of Lombardy

118–27 In the Ten Years' War, Milan virtually destroys Como.

164 The Veronese League is formed to prevent Emperor Frederick Barbarossa bringing the Lombard cities under his control. It forms the basis of the Lombard League, established in 1167.

176 Frederick Barbarossa is defeated by the Lombard League at Legnano. By the Peace of Constance in 1183, he is forced to accept the independence of the city states as free communes.

262 The rise of the Scaligeri family of Garda begins when Mastino I della Scala becomes mayor of Verona, the first Scaligeri to rise to a position of prominence in the Garda region.

277 Mastino I della Scala is murdered, but the Venetians immediately replace him with his tyrannical brother, Alberto.

278–1447 The Visconti in power in Milan.

311–29 Cangrande I della Scala extends his sphere of influence.

335 The Visconti take over Como.

352 The hated Cangrande II della Scala assumes power, and is murdered seven years later by his brother Cansignorio.

387 Scaligeri rule comes to an end when Verona is besieged by the Visconti.

405–1521 Venice conquers Brescia, Verona and Lake Garda.

450 Francesco Sforza, son-in-law of the last Visconti, assumes power in Milan and Como.

496–1500 The area of modern-day Ticino is annexed to Switzerland.

500–25 Milan is a bone of contention between France, Germany and Venice. Emperor Charles V installs another Sforza as duke.

535 After the death of the last Sforza duke, Milan falls to Spain.

1796 Napoleon conquers Lombardy and the Veneto. One year later the Cisalpine Republic is formed at the Treaty of Campoformio.

1814–15 Napoleon is defeated. At the Congress of Vienna, Lombardy and the Veneto are ceded to Austria.

Early 19th century The Italians of the north under Austrian rule and the 'free' Italians of the kingdom of Piedmont begin to campaign for an independent Italy. In 1842, a newspaper called *Il Risorgimento* (*The Awakening*) is published, after which the independence movement takes its name. It is led by Giuseppe Garibaldi.

1848–66 The Risorgimento fights against Austrian rule.

1859 After losing several of their early battles, the freedom fighters gain a decisive victory at the bloody Battle of Solferino, south of Lake Garda.

1861 Vienna is forced to surrender Lombardy and the Veneto to the new Kingdom of Italy.

1919 Under the terms of the Treaty of Saint-Germain, Austria loses the northern shore of lake Garda, the Trentino and also the southern Tyrol. Reunified Italy now extends as far as the Brenner Pass. Benito Mussolini establishes the first fascist brigades in Milan. The fascists come to power three years later.

1943–45 After the collapse of the northern front, Mussolini retires to Lake Garda and founds the short-lived 'Republic of Salò'. On 28 April 1945 the Duce and his mistress Clara Petacci are caught by partisans while trying to flee to Switzerland, and are summarily executed.

1946 Italy becomes a republic.

1993 Catastrophic floods at Lake Maggiore.

1996 A centre-left coalition (*Ulivo*) wins local and regional elections.

1998 Following a government crisis caused by the communists, D'Alema takes over as prime minister.

Taking the high road

Smile from Val Cannobina

Route 1

Lake Maggiore

Lake Maggiore, the *Lacus Verbanus* of Ancient Rom
much praised as a natural wonder and a popular holida
destination for generations, is for many the epitome of t
South, of *Bella Italia*. Like all the lakes south of the Alp
Lake Maggiore owes its existence to Ice Age glacie
which hollowed out its base to a depth of 372m (1,220
– or a full 179m (587ft) below sea-level. With a surfac
area of 216sq m (2,324sq ft), Lake Maggiore is the se
ond-largest of the Northern Italian Lakes after Lake Gard
it is 66km (41 miles) long, but has an average width of b
tween 4km (2 miles) and 11km (6 miles). The lake's mo
important river is the Ticino, which has its source in t
Alps of Central Switzerland and flows into Lake Maggio
near Locarno. The Ticino river also drains the lake, flow
ing into the Po not far from Pavia.

Lake Maggiore is shared by Italy and Switzerland: t
upper fifth of it is Swiss and forms part of the canton
Ticino; the western shore is part of the Italian region
Piedmont (province of Novara); and the eastern sho
belongs to Lombardy (province of Varese). The nort
ern part of the lake, surrounded by high mountains suc
as the Gridone (2,188m/7,180ft), opens up more and mo
towards the south, unveiling its special attractions as
does so. The mountains form a grand backdrop, and t
southern sun bathes the landscape in brilliant light.

But Lake Maggiore isn't just sunshine, water and mou
tains: its villas and parks, now magnificent museums, a
reminders of the old days when people travelled from M
lan to the lake by coach, and travel was the privilege
a small section of society. Today all that pomp an

Preceding pages: Lake Orta

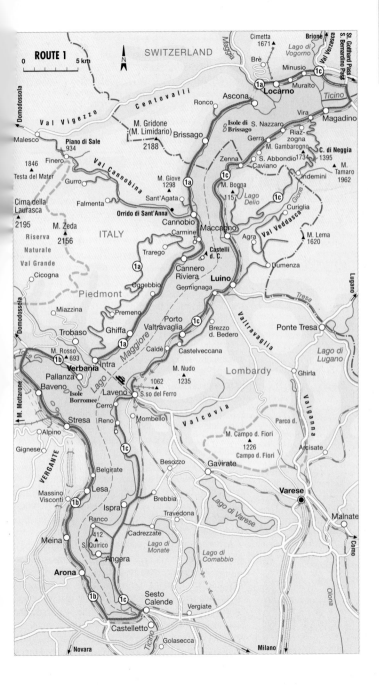

grandeur is history; increasing traffic and industry mak[...]
smog-free days something of a rarity.

With its towns of Locarno, Ascona, Verbania and Stres[...]
the Piedmont shore is more wealthy than the less devel[...]
oped eastern shore. The latter, on the other hand, has mor[...]
unspoilt natural scenery. The prosperity of the wester[...]
shore means no less than a third of the working popula[...]
tion on the eastern shore of Lake Maggiore work in Switz[...]
erland, and commute between the two countries daily.

1a – The Western Shore

Locarno – Ascona – Brissago – Cannobio – Verbania
(57km/35 miles) *See map, p15*

Lakeshore at Locarno

★★ **Locarno** (pop. 17,000) vies with Lugano for the ti-
tle of finest town in the Ticino. The magnificent landscape
at the upper end of Lake Maggiore and the mild, fog-free
climate attracted Northern European tourists here from the
end of the 19th century onwards. The town prospered after World War II, and now includes the suburbs of Muralto, Minusio, Orselina and Brione. Today the shore of
Lake Maggiore is built up from the Maggia to the Verza-
sca, but Locarno still retains much of its charm – a special combination of Swiss-Alpine and Southern-Italian.

The region round Locarno was probably inhabited during prehistoric times, but was certainly settled during the
Roman era. The first written mention of the town dates
from AD789. Over the centuries, Locarno profited from
its strategic location at the northern end of Lake Maggiore,
on the trading route leading across the great Alpine passes.
It received its charter from the emperor Barbarossa in
1189, and passed into the hands of the Viscontis of Milan in 1342. In 1513 it was conquered by the Swiss Confederation, and after the fall of the Ancien Regime (1798)
it became a part of the Swiss canton of Lugano. From 1803
to 1878 it then shared the status as Ticino's capital alter-
nately with Lugano and Bellinzona. The town became
famous from the Treaty of Locarno, signed in 1925, which
allowed Germany back into the League of Nations after
World War I.

Aspects of the Piazza Grande

At the centre of Locarno is the **Piazza Grande**, where
the traditional weekly market is held every second Tuesday; the square dates from the 19th century. The 14th-cen-
tury Torre del Comune forms part of the line of houses
on the side facing the mountains; to the east is the municipal park with the theatre. Down the Via Franchino
Rusca is the ★ **Castello**, still one of the most important
castles in the Ticino despite being largely destroyed by the
Confederation in 1532. It was founded in medieval times,
and today houses the **Museo Civico** (April to October
Tuesday to Sunday 10am–noon, 2–5pm) with its exten-

ve collections of local archaeological finds and Romanesque sculpture. The historic town centre is a great ace for a stroll: one of the finest townhouses is the **Casa usca**, which contains the Pinacoteca Comunale (daily cept Monday 10am–noon and 2–5pm, Thursday to)pm) with the important Dada collection by Hans Arp.

Of the churches in the old town, **Santa Maria in Selva** well known for its Late Gothic ★ choir frescoes, show-g *Scenes from the Life of Christ*, but the most famous sa-ed structure on the northern shore of Lake Maggiore definitely the church of ★★ **San Vittore** in Muralto, not r from the railway station. This three-aisled Romanesque lared basilica dates from between 1090 and 1110, and e Romanesque ★★ crypt with its fascinating capitals definitely worth a visit.

Monk at Madonna del Sasso

Above Locarno stands the famous pilgrimage church **Madonna del Sasso**, the site of which doubles as a perb observation point for the city, mountains and lake. can be reached by road or by tram, or, for the more en-getic, by the old Way of the Cross. The present pil-image church of Santa Maria Assunta dates from the th and 17th centuries, and the main attraction of the terior is Bramantino's *Flight from Egypt* (1520).

Hidden Ascona

e mighty delta of the Maggia separates Locarno from e no less beautiful town of ★ **Ascona** (pop. 4,800). Still ly a small fishing village before the turn of the cen-ry, Ascona first became a paradise for theosophical eekers after truth' before becoming the cosmopolitan re-rt it is today. Picturesquely situated in a bay, the town s an unmistakeable flair of its own, despite the annual urist invasion. The parish church of **SS Pietro e Paolo**, 6th-century three-aisled pillared basilica, contains three agnificent ★ altar paintings by the local painter Giovanni rodine (1594–1630), who lived next door in Ascona's est baroque building, the ★ **Casa Borrani** (1620). At e edge of the old town centre is the **Collegio Paio**, unded in 1584, with a fine Renaissance courtyards and nagnificent ★ cloister. The church of **Santa Maria della isericordia** contains several valuable ★ frescoes dating om the 15th and 16th centuries.

Collegio Paio: the cloister

High above Ascona is **Monte Verità** (321m/1,050ft), th a view across the lake and the Maggia delta. The **Casa natta** (April to October Tuesday to Sunday 2.30–6pm, ly to August 3–7pm), headquarters of the 'Vegetarian operative of Ascona' from 1900 to 1920, contains much formation on all the reformists and communards who me here to 'get away from it all' earlier this century.

The nearby town of **Brissago** has a very southern at-osphere, with all its palazzi and Mediterranean vege-ion. Archaeological finds in the vicinity point to early

Casa Anatta exhibits

settlement by the Celts, who were followed by the Romans. During the Middle Ages, Brissago was a miniature republic and enjoyed several privileges such as tax exemption and its own legal system – rights which had to be fiercely defended during the 16th and 17th centuries after it had joined the Confederation. Today, tourism is Brissago's main source of income, and the historic centre is consequently losing much of its former charm. Sights worth seeing include the **Casa Branca** (1680–1720) with its magnificent facade; the church of ★ **Madonna del Ponte** (1520–45) just to the south of the town, a fine example of Lombardian architecture; and the famous **cigar factory** (Fabbrica Tabacchi) founded in 1847, also south of the town (guided tours from May to September).

Madonna del Ponte

The region around Brissago is ideal for hiking, with some fine views of the lake and the mighty massif of the Gridone (2,188m/7,180ft) in the distance. Don't miss the ★ **Brissago Islands**, either. They were probably inhabited as far back as Roman times, and a ruined church on the Isolino (the smaller island) dates from the 12th century. The Isola Grande has a magnificent ★ **botanical garden** (guided tours April to September), with some unique tropical and subtropical vegetation. The villa, built in Italian Renaissance style in 1927, today houses an art museum (daily 9.30am–5.30pm).

Ferry to Isola Grande

Across the border in Italy, **Cannobio** is a delightful place with a historic centre, picturesque arcades next to the lake and the pilgrimage church of **Santa Pietà** adjacent to the quayside. Built according to the plans of Pellegrino Tibaldi in 1571, it contains a miracle-working image of the *Mourning of Christ*. The 13th-century **Palazzo delle Ragione**, the old town hall, houses a small local museum.

Market day in Cannobio

Barely 2km (1½ miles) from the town centre, the annnobino stream crashes through the wild ★ **Orrido ant'Anna** gorge. Slicing between the Gridone and Monte eda, the ★★ **Val Cannobina** itself is well worth a detour, ith tiny settlements and the occasional church clinging the mountainsides. Up this valley, a curiosity of a very pecial kind is the village of **Gurro**, whose inhabitants an be proud of their Scottish ancestry. After the Battle f Pavia in 1525, a company of Scottish mercenaries fight-g on the side of the French decided to flee to this remote alley, where they settled down to a life of mountain farm-ng and married the local girls. Even today, the local di-lect contains elements of the gaelic tongue, and kilts re worn at festivals. Further evidence of the Scottish in-uence is to be found in the **museum** at Gurro (daily ex-ept Thursday 9am–5pm), as well as in the names of such stablishments as the **Scotch Bar** and **Ristorante Scozia**.

Val Cannobina

Continuing down the western shore, just before the pop-ular resort of Cannero Riviera, two rocky islands, the **Castelli di Cannero**, jut out of the water. They were once the stronghold of the notorious Mazzarditi brothers, who took over the existing castles on the islands in the early 15th century and terrorised lake travellers and lakeside dwellers with their piracy. The castles were razed to the ground in 1414 by Filippo Visconti; only the ruins remain.

From **Cannero Riviera** it is possible to take the moun-tain road to Verbania via Trarego, the Passo della Piazza and Premeno, but this route is only recommended for ex-perienced mountain drivers. The route along the shore, which continues through **Oggebbio** and **Ghiffa**, has its own wonderful panoramas, including, over on the eastern shore, the cliffs of **Rocca di Caldè** (*see page 24*).

19

1b – The Piedmont Shore

Verbania – Baveno – Stresa – Lake Orta – Arona – Sesto Calende (91km/57 miles) *See map, p20*

The Piedmont shore of Lake Maggiore is definitely the most cultural and traditional one, as evidenced by its many villas. It is proud to have been visited by many well-known historical figures, including Queen Victoria.

The town of ★ **Verbania** (pop. 31,000) derives its name from the original Roman name for the lake: *Lacus Ver-banus*. The two main sections of the town are Intra and ★ **Pallanza**; the former is rather industrial, while the lat-ter is cosmopolitan, and one of the best known resorts on the lake. Pallanza, delightfully situated at the foot of the Monte Rosso, is separated from Intra by the Punta della

Pallanza: blooms in Villa Taranto

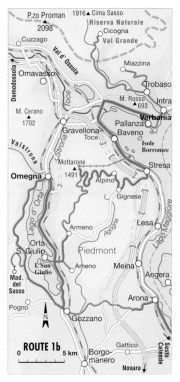

Castagnola and also by the large park surround ing the ★★ **Villa Taranto** (daily April to Octo ber 8.30am–7.30pm). This park is one enormou botanical garden, containing one of the richest co lections of subtropical flora in Italy. Rhododer dron, beech, tulips, magnolia, dahlias, azaleas a grow here in profusion among the leaping foun tains. The park originally belonged to a Scottis nobleman, Neil McEacharn, who bequeathed it the Italian state on his death in 1964.

The most important structure in Pallanza it self lies north of the Borgo, or old town, on th Viale G A Azari: the church of ★ **Madonna d Campagna**. Originally built 'in the fields', th church's original beauty has been somewha marred today by industrial buildings nearby. Orig inally Romanesque, the church underwent Re naissance alteration during the early 16th centur The octagonal cupola with its pillared gallery an unusual feature, and the Romanesque cam panile is also striking. Highlights inside the build ing include choir stalls dating from 1582 and als several 16th-century frescoes.

The landscape around Verbania is a good ex ample of just how varied the Italian lake region i Just a few miles from the crowded lake prome nade, the magnificent valleys and mountains ar breathtakingly peaceful. The summit of the Mont Rosso (693m/2,273ft) with its view across the Gulf o Borromeo can very nearly be reached by car along a na row road from the Viale G A Azari. ★ **Monte Zed** (2,156m/7,070ft) near Miazzina provides an even mor impressive panorama.

Lake Maggiore's so-called 'riviera' extends from Ver bania around the Bay of Borromeo as far as Stresa. Thi fertile strip of land with its profusion of subtropical veg etation is best visited in early spring or late autumn whe there are less tourists around; the views in clear weathe can extend as far as the Swiss Alps at these times of yea

The pinkish granite quarried near the town of ★ **Baven** (pop. 4,500) was used in the construction of St Paul' Basilica in Rome and the Galleria Vittorio Emanuele in Milan. Baveno's Romanesque parish church an octagonal Renaissance baptistery are worth a visit, and th town is also famous as a health spa: Queen Victoria, Crow Prince Frederick, the later German emperors and Richar Wagner all stayed here at different times.

The promenade in Baveno provides unique views of th famous ★★ **Borromean Islands.** These four islands be

Borromean Islands from Baveno

veen Baveno, Stresa and Pallanza still exert a magic attraction. The **Isola Bella** in particular has been praised y scores of writers and poets, including Dumas and Stendl. The magic of the Isola Bella is definitely man-made, wever: the idea of shaping the rocky island into a ship uld have come straight from the Walt Disney workshop. was Antonio Crivelli from Ponte Tresa, however, who rned the island into a complete work of art on the orer of Carlo Borromeo III and his wife Isabella d'Abba. he **Palazzo Borromeo** (daily April to October 9am–noon d 1.30–5.30pm), partly designed by Carlo Fontana, conins several majestic halls and also the famous grottoes.

Isola Bella: the baroque park

he terraced ★ **baroque park** is the real highlight, however, with its delightful mix of subtropical flora and white eacocks; the dream-like beauty of the whole place is arred only by all the kitsch and souvenirs on sale. The ola dei Pescatori, despite some fine flora, is rather the orse for wear, with its narrow streets and very expensive afood restaurants. The **Isola Madre** – the largest of the ur islands – has some fine vegetation and also a stylh 16th-century Palazzo Borromeo containing an intersting ceramics collection (daily April to October am–noon and 1.30–5.30pm). The fourth island, the **Isola an Giovanni**, is privately owned.

21

Stresa (pop. 5,000), one of the most elegant resorts in aly during the 19th century, is rather past its prime to-ay. Nevertheless, many of the grand hotels still retain me of their former splendour from the days when rowned heads, famous artists and wealthy aristocrats ere regular visitors; the American author Ernest Hemgway wrote his novel *Another Country* here. The view cross the lake from the *Lungolago* (promenade) is a ust: it takes in the Borromean Islands and also the opsite shore of Lake Maggiore as far as Monte Tamaro.

here are several good excursion possibilities around resa. Just outside the town on the road to Arona is the **Villa Pallavicino** (April to October 9am–6pm) with s enormous park and zoo. For the energetic, the mountnous countryside between Lake Maggiore and Lake Orta as many numbered hiking routes – and if the weather gets et, why not visit the ★ **Umbrella Museum** in Gignese April to September Tuesday to Sunday 10am–noon and –6pm). The summit of the ★ **Monte Mottarone** (1,491m/ 891ft) above Stresa is a famous observation point, and an be reached by a toll road with several hairpins.

Villa Pallavicino

luch overshadowed by Lake Maggiore is the far smaller **Lake Orta** in Piedmont. The Lago d'Orta was known the Romans as *Lacus Cusius*, and is 13km (8 miles) long,

Basilica di San Giulio, details

*Statue at
Sacro Monte*

an average of 1.5km (1 mile) wide and measures 143r (470ft) at its deepest point. The steep alpine ranges of Val strona and Val d'Ossola form a spectacular contrast t the rolling green hills below.

Romantically situated on the lake is ★ **Orta San Giuli** (294m/964ft; pop. 1,200). The baroque buildings aroun the central piazza are charming, but the real highlight i the small ★ **Isola di San Giulio** out in the lake, just hectares (7 acres) in size, and dominated by the forme episcopal palace and the ★ **Basilica di San Giulio**. Orig inally founded in around 390, today's structure is pre dominantly Romanesque. Don't miss the 12th-centur black marble ★★ pulpit, still in excellent condition. An other sacred site in this region is the Franciscan monaster on the ★ **Sacro Monte** of Orta. There is a magnificent view from up here across the western bank of Lake Orta, an the outline of the 18th-century pilgrimage church o Madonna del Sasso can be made out in the distance.

From the southern shore of the lake it's not far to **Aron** (pop. 16,000), with its colossal ★ **statue** (20m/62ft high of its most famous son, San Carlo Borromeo, looking ou across Lake Maggiore. Cardinal Borromeo (1538–84), a ardent advocate of Catholicism, was canonised in 161C this statue of him dates from 1697, and if you go up th spiral stairway and ladder inside you can look out of hi eyes across the lake as far as the Varesotto.

At the southern end of Lake Maggiore is the industria town of **Sesto Calende** (pop. 10,000), known to the Ro mans as *Sextum Calendarum*, and usually driven throug very rapidly by most people today. The region was pop ulated very early on, however, and fascinating archaeo logical finds dating from the 9th century BC and earlie can be examined in the **Museo Civico** (Tuesday to Sat urday 8.30am–noon and 3–5pm, Sunday 10am–noon an 3–7pm). Sesto Calende isn't all industrial either – try vis iting the ★ **Parco della Valle del Ticino**, a green oasi where the region's original natural scenery is still intac The Ticino river leaves Lake Maggiore here, and innu merable species of bird (especially herons and swallows nest along its banks.

*Sesto Calende:
Parco della Valle del Ticino*

1c – The Lombardian Shore

Sesto Calende – Angera – Laveno – Luino – Maccagn – Val Veddasca (80km/50miles) *See map, p15*

The eastern, Lombardian shore of Lake Maggiore is fa removed from such noble resorts as Ascona or Stresa, an gardens and parks here are conspicuous by their absence The eastern shore may be less spectacular, but it's fa

Santa Caterina del Sasso

ess spoilt and more rugged. The towns and small villages have so far successfully managed to escape the clutches of tourism, and are still largely owned by the local population. The hinterland is flat as far as Laveno, with several small communities dotted around, and further north the shore of the lake gets much steeper, becoming alpine in character but without losing that special Mediterranean character that makes Lake Maggiore so unique.

Angera (pop. 5,500), just 8km (5 miles) from Sesto Calende (*see page 22*), is a busy town situated in a pretty bay opposite Arona. The main highlight here is easily spotted: the ★ **Rocca di Angera** (April to October 9.30am–12.30pm and 2–6pm, July and August 9.30am–12.30pm and 3–7pm), a proud fortress up on a hill behind the town, with a commanding view across the countryside and the lake. The site is steeped in history: not far from the fortress is the cave known as the Antro di Mitra, where traces of the Mithraic cult (1st and 2nd centuries AD) were discovered. The castle dates back to the Torriani and the Visconti (14th century), and there are some fine ★ frescoes (1314) in the Gothic Sala della Giustizia depicting a Visconti victory. Don't forget to climb the tower – the view across to the Sacro Monte near Varese (*see page 15*) and the small island of Partegora is impressive.

Signposts along the eastern shore, not far from the tiny village of **Reno**, point the way to a place of pilgrimage: ★ **Santa Caterina del Sasso**. A 12th-century chapel on the site became a small Dominican monastery, which was miraculously spared destruction in the 17th century when a landslide stopped within feet of the church. The site immediately became a place of pilgrimage, but its guardian angels deserted it 270 years later in 1910 when another landslide smashed through the church roof. The church and the small monastery are at their most impressive when viewed from the lake.

Santa Caterina del Sasso: ceiling detail

From **Laveno** (pop. 9,000) there's a good view acro
the Gulf of Borromeo to the peaks of the Valais Alp
The town itself is industrial, but the local ceramic trad
has a long history. In Cerro (3km/2 miles out of Laven
the Civica Raccolta di Terraglia museum documents th
development of this craft, introduced to the region in 1850

Beyond Laveno is the 'Alpine' part of the eastern shor
the terrain gets steeper, and the narrow road starts goin
through several tunnels. Soon Castelveccana comes int
view, along with the famous steep rock known as th
Rocca di Caldè (373m/1,220ft). A castle once stood o
top of the rock; it was razed by Confederation troops i
1513. Just before **Porto Valtravaglia** (pop. 2,500), whic
lies right beside the lake, there's an interesting alterna
tive route (good views) via the villages of Nasca
Musadino and Muceno to **Brezzo di Bedero**. Brezza'
12th-century church of San Vittore still retains severa
of its Romanesque features.

Luino

Luino lies at the point where the valleys of the Tresa and
the Travaglia meet Lake Maggiore, and is the industrial
centre of the Lombardian shore. Luino's main attraction
is its market, held every Wednesday. The area between the
Piazza Garibaldi and the lake promenade is filled with
all manner of fascinating wares for sale. Luino is thought
to have been the birthplace of the Renaissance artist
Bernadino Luini (1480–1532), but those expecting to see
any works by the great painter here in Luino will be dis-
appointed. The church of **San Pietro** in Campagna does
have an *Adoration of the Magi* attributed to him, however.
The Museo Civico in the Viale Dante contains several prehistoric finds from the region.

Hiking enthusiasts will enjoy the region around Luino,
especially the ★ **Monte Lema** (1,620m/5,310ft) on the
border with Ticino. There are marked routes from Du-
menza and Curiglia to the summit. Motorists who don't
mind hairpin bends can also travel as far as the Rifugio
Campiglio (1,184m/3,884ft), from which the summit is
only another 1½-hr hike. The view of Lakes Lugano and
Maggiore from up here in good weather is superb.

Val Veddasca vernacular

At the confluence of the Veddasca Valley lies the resort
of **Maccagno**, separated into upper and lower sections
by the Giona stream. Apart from the lake, there are numerous excursion possibilities, including the scenic ★ **Val
Veddasca**. The winding valley road leads to the almost
deserted village of ★ **Indemni** just over the Swiss border, whose picturesque alleys and stone-roofed houses be-
lie the fact that depopulation is a real problem in this part
of the world. There are superb views as the road snakes its
way down to **Vira** back on the lake.

Lake-Hopping

Laveno – Varese – Como (48km/29 miles)

This connecting route between Lakes Maggiore and Como has several hidden attractions: the delightful Lake Varese, for instance, surrounded by attractive rolling hills; the provincial capital of Varese with its magnificent Sacro Monte; several fine mountain views; and Arcumeggia, a village that has become a very original art gallery. Plan a day for this trip.

Arcumeggia fresco

The first interesting detour on the route comes a few miles beyond Laveno: the little village of ★ **Arcumeggia**, where contemporary Italian artists have been busy reviving the ancient art of fresco painting. There are around 170 different frescoes on the houses here, and the place is well worth a visit. This region, known as the Valcuvia, has several other attractions: the 16th-century **Villa Bozzolo** in Casalzuigno with its magnificent park, the Romanesque campanile of **San Lorenzo** in the village of Cuveglio, and the ruined Sforza fortress above Orino on the northern slopes of the Monte Campo dei Fiori.

25

Going out in Gavirate

Travel on now via Gemonio (Romanesque church with frescoes) to **Gavirate** (pop. 8,000), picturesquely situated on the northern shore of **Lake Varese**. This 8-km (5-mile) long lake measures 4km (2 miles) at its widest point, and is extremely shallow (max depth 26m/85ft); its banks are thus rather marshy and this has spared it much new building construction. Wine is grown on the hills at the foot of **Monte Campo dei Fiori** (1,226m/4,020ft) and also

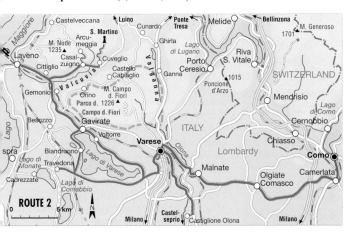

ROUTE 2   0 _____ 5km

in the region south of the lake. To the southwest of lak Varese are two smaller lakes: Lake Comabbio and Lak Monate. A third one, Lake Biandronno, is almost com pletely dry now. Several remains of prehistoric lak dwellings have been discovered in this region, and finc can be seen in the **Museo Preistorico** (June to Septem ber Thursday to Sunday 3–6pm) on the tiny island o **Virgina** in Lake Varese, not far from Biandronno.

Fishing on Virgina

There are several fine cultural sights in the Lake Vares region, especially in **Voltorre** (2km/1½ miles from Gavi rate), where the parish church of **San Michele** has a su perb 12th-century Romanesque ★ cloister, and also i **Travedona** (7km/4 miles southwest of Gavirate on Lak Monate), with its church of **Santa Maria della Neve**.

The provincial capital of **Varese** (pop. 95,000) was stil quite insignificant during the Middle Ages, but has now developed into a typically Northern Italian metropolis wit a lot of industry but also a lot of old villas and parks. Varese lies in the region known as the Varesotto, which extends from Lake Lugano up to the edge of Greater Milan, and includes the famous Sacro Monte, Castiglione Olona and Castelseprio.

Unlike Como, the originally Gallo-Roman settlemen of Varese hardly played any role in Lombard history; it only became a town in 1816. One of the most noticeable features of the town is the baroque campanile (77m/252ft) of the basilica of **San Vittore**, built between 1580 and 1615; the original Renaissance structure was given a neo classical facade in 1788. The building contains frescoes by leading Lombard masters, and the neighbouring ★ **bap tistery** has several fresco fragments dating from the 13th and 14th centuries.

The old part of Varese is centred around San Vittore, but there's a sharp contrast just a short distance away in the Piazza Monte Grappa, where buildings dating from 1927 to 1935 all bear the unmistakeable stamp of Italian Fascist architecture. Northwest of the square, up the Via Sacco, is the 18th-century Austrian style **Palazzo Estense** (1776–83), reminiscent of Schoenbrunn in Vienna. Its owner, Francesco III d'Este, was the imperial governor of Austrian Lombardy and also Duke of Modena. Across the grounds in the **Villa Mirabello**, the Municipal Museum (Tuesday to Saturday 9.30am–noon and 2–5pm, Sunday 9am–12.30pm) contains an interesting prehistoric col lection and also an art gallery.

Varese: Palazzo Estense

One very good excursion from Varese is to the ★ **Sacro Monte** (880m/2,880ft) or 'Holy Mountain', a famous place of pilgrimage. A pilgrimage church was built on the

ountain in the 10th century, and it was later used to house
statue of the Virgin, known as the Black Madonna be-
ause it is carved from dark wood. In the 16th century,
ans were drawn up for a ★ **Via Crucis** (Way of the
ross), lined with chapels. Thanks to the skills of the ar-
hitect Giuseppe Bernascone, who built the round domed
tructures at the beginning of the 17th century, the as-
ent along the 2-km (1½-mile) long cobbled route lead-
ng from the Prima Cappella to the church of Santa Maria
el Monte is unforgettable. Art and landscape are har-
noniously combined, and the chapels are decorated with
nany frescoes and several larger-than-life terracotta fig-
res. The church of **Santa Maria del Monte** itself, in
vhich the Black Madonna still stands, is a mixture of styles
rom Romanesque to baroque; its massive campanile is
articularly striking, and the early 11th-century crypt con-
ains some fine Gothic frescoes.

*Sacro Monte: Way of the Cross
and Santa Maria del Monte*

While in Varese, don't miss an excursion 11km (6 miles)
southwards to ★★ **Castiglione Olona** (churches and museum Tuesday to Friday 10am–noon and 3–6pm, weekend 10am–12.30pm and 2.30–6pm), which today is a small
and rather insignificant industrial town. During the Renaissance, however, it was turned into a kind of 'mini-Florence' in the middle of Lombardy by Cardinal Branda
Castiglione (1350–1443). The numerous palazzi, including that of the cardinal himself, have lost much of their
former glory, but the sacred buildings are magnificent. The
★ **Chiesa di Villa** (1422–43) is a centralised structure reminiscent of Brunelleschi's work in Florence, and the ★ **Col-
legiata**, reached by an idyllic walk, contains marvellous
frescoes by the Florentine artist Masolino da Panicale
(1435), who also painted the *Scenes from the Life of John
the Baptist* in the ★ baptistery.

Castiglione Olona

Not far away, at ★ **Castelseprio**, the large excavation site
to the east of the village was probably a settlement founded
by the Celtic Insubrians, then the capital of a Lombard
province, and then a powerful medieval commune before its destruction by the Visconti in 1287. Several ruined
walls have been exposed to view. The small church of
Santa Maria Foris Portas nearby probably dates from the
7th century originally, and contains a magnificent ★ fresco
cycle which, though incomplete, was painted somewhere
between the 7th and 9th centuries.

To reach Lake Como from Varese, take the SS 342 via
Malnate and Olgiate-Comasco. The most common type
of building along this route is unfortunately the *super-
mercado*, but there's an interesting coach, steam train
and bicycle museum in the Villa Rachele-Ogliari in **Malnate**, to add a welcome touch of nostalgia.

The lake from a Swiss perspective

Route 3

Lake Lugano

Lake Lugano is 271m (889ft) above sea-level, and mea sures 48.9sq km (19sq miles); three quarters of the lake l in Ticino. With its strange shape and steep, rocky shore Lake Lugano is rather reminiscent of Lake Lucerne m nus the Alpine backdrop. The best view of the lake, whic has an average width of less than 2km (1½ miles) can b had from the hills around Lugano, but for a proper ex perience of the *Ceresio*, as the locals refer to their lak take a boat trip past the rocky mountain slopes. Unlik Lakes Como or Maggiore, the large amount of weed i Lake Lugano means that its dark-green water never ap pears transparent, even on sunny days.

Route 3a: Lugano to Como

Lugano – Melide – Morcote – Bissone– Capolago Riva San Vitale – Mendrisio (32km/20 miles)

Lugano waterfront

★★ **Lugano** (pop. 29,000), the largest city in Ticino, magnificently situated in its semicircular bay betwee the peaks of **Monte Brè** (925m/3,034ft) in the east an **Monte Salvatore** (912m/2,992ft) in the south. The won derful mixture of stunning mountain scenery and mil sunny climate has made the region around Lugano on of the most popular tourist areas in Switzerland, thoug the sheer speed of construction work during the pa decades has also resulted in quite a number of negativ developments.

Archaeological finds date the earliest settlement of th region back to pre-Roman times. The city received its fir written mention (as *Luano*) in the year 818. During the Middle Ages Lugano was often involved in the struggles between Milan and Como. From 1803 to 1978 it alternated as the capital of Ticino with Bellinzona and Locarno.

The best place to start any tour of the city is the **Piazza della Riforma** with its elegant 19th-century buildings. The cafés here are popular meeting-places for young and old alike. The **Municipio**, or Town Hall, on the south side of the piazza dates from 1844, and the famous lake promenades lead southwards and eastwards towards Paradiso and the municipal park. Inland is the largely traffic-free city centre, where several old buildings still survive. The Via Pessina has picturesque arcades and typical cobblestones, and the Via Nassa, which joins it to the south, has now become the city's main shopping street. It comes out in the Piazza B Luini, named after the Renaissance painter several of whose works can be admired here in the church of ★★ **Santa Maria degli Angioli**. Built in 1515, the church belonged to a Franciscan monastery that was dissolved in 1848. The interior is dominated by Luini's enormous *Crucifixion*, which he completed in 1529 while under the influence of Leonardo da Vinci. Three other frescoes – the *Last Supper* on the south wall, and the *Mourning of Christ* and *Mary with Jesus and St John* – were originally painted by Luini for the monastery.

Encounters on the piazza

Santa Maria degli Angioli

29

High above the old town is the ★ **Cathedral of San Lorenzo**. First mentioned as a parish church in 818, it dates back to an old Roman pillared basilica that was vaulted and extended in the 13th century before receiving its side

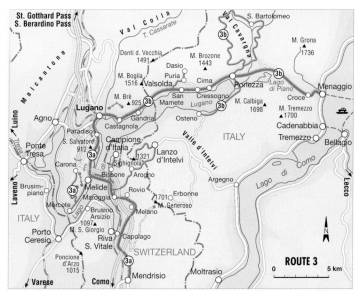

ROUTE 3

0   5 km

Villa Favorita

Morcote

Swiss Miniature

chapels in the 18th century and much interior renovation. The ★ Renaissance facade (1500–17) is a very attractive sight with its three portals, richly carved figures and round window, and is considered one of the finest examples of Lombard Renaissance architecture in all Ticino.

Don't miss the city's museums either, especially the **Museo Cantonale d'Arte** (Palazzo Reali, Via Canova 10, Wednesday to Sunday 10am–5pm, Tuesday 2–5pm) and the Museo Cantonale di Storia Naturale. Until a short time ago, the Thyssen-Bornemisza collection of paintings in the famous **Villa Favorita** in Castagnola is a must for all art lovers. Much of the original collection was transferred to Madrid in 1992. Now the villa contains works by 19th- and 20th-century American and European artists.

Melide is a popular holiday resort with a special attraction: the 1:25 scale models collectively known as ★ **Swiss Miniature** (9am–7pm; July and August 9am–10pm), representing the most important sights of Switzerland (towns, buildings, etc.).

A cable railway leads up from the lake to ★ **Carona**, a picturesque mountain village with several attractive churches. From here it's possible to hike along the mountain to the next destination on the route, the village of ★★ **Morcote**, one of the most popular excursion destinations in the region. Even though it was discovered by the tourist industry quite early on, Morcote has successfully retained much of its historic substance. The village blends in harmoniously with its surroundings, and this has made it a magnet for visitors. A flight of steps laid out in 1732 leads up to the terraced cemetery and the parish church of ★ **Santa Maria del Sasso**, built in the 13th century; inside there are several magnificent Renaissance frescoes. The free-standing campanile dates from 1539.

Near the village of **Bissone** is the Ponte Diga, built in 1844, which takes rail and road traffic across the narrowest part of the lake. Bissone is famous as the home of several famous families of artists such as Borromini, Maderno and Tencalla. Its most famous son was the architect Francesco Borromini (1599–1667), the biggest rival of Gian Lorenzo Bernini in Rome. Bissone does not possess even one of the master's works, however.

At the southern end of Lake Lugano is **Capolago**, which used to be an important trading centre before the Gotthard railway was built, and was fortified by the Visconti. It is the birthplace of architect Carlo Maderna (1556–1629), who built the facade of St Peter's in Rome. Capolago is the starting-point for tours to ★★**Monte Generoso** (1,701m/5,580ft); in good weather the mountain panorama from the top extends from Monte Viso (3,841m/12,600ft) to the Bernina (4,049m/13,280ft). Early summer, when the flowers are all in bloom, is the best time to take the rack railway to the top.

31

Creeper in Riva San Vitale

The small town of **Riva San Vitale** (pop. 2,000) is most famous for its Early Christian baptistery and the domed church of Santa Croce. Inhabited as long ago as prehistoric times, and first mentioned as *Sobenno* in 774, during medieval times Riva San Vitale was one of Como's bases in its war against Milan. The town is dominated by the mighty dome of ★★**Santa Croce**, one of the finest churches in Switzerland. It was built between 1588 and 1592 by the architect Giovanni Antonio Piotto, from Varallo in the Mendrisiotto. Despite sharing several characteristics with contemporary centralised structures (e.g. Todi, Montepulciano), the building also presages the Baroque era. Eight mighty columns support the huge dome crowned with its lantern. The fresco decoration, with its many strange figures and gargoyle-like Mannerist faces, is also very impressive.

Riva San Vitale's second claim to fame is its ★★**Baptistery of San Giovanni**, beside the parish church of San Vitale. The centralised structure with its octagonal cupola was built in around 500, and originally had a square ambulatory (some parts of the original roof still survive in the western wall). The eastern apse probably dates from the Carolingian period; the fresco remains showing the *Crucifixion* have been dated to around 1000; and the paintings in the niches to the left and right of the apse date from the 14th and 15th centuries. Sections of the artistically paved marble floor also survive; the octagonal *piscina* in the pavement was originally used for total-immersion baptisms before the erection of the enormous baptism stone (2m/7ft across). The municipal museum in Riva also

San Giovanni

Cosma e Damiano in Mendrisio

contains an interesting exhibition of works by the 19th century 'mountain painter' Giovanni Segantini.

From Riva, continue to **Mendrisio** (pop. 7,000), a lively town which has retained its old *Borgo*, several churches and numerous palazzi despite a lot of busy construction work. The Easter processions here are famed far beyond the borders of Ticino, and are a very colourful affair. The old town centre is dominated by the parish church of **SS Cosma e Damiano**, a monumental centralised structure dating from the 19th century with an octagonal dome. The former monastery church of San Giovanni Battista was built above a previous structure between 1722 and 1738; it contains some marvellous stucco and also several *trompe l'oeil* ceiling paintings. Mendrisio also possesses one of the most magnificent baroque palazzi in Ticino: the **Palazzo Pollini** (1719–21).

From Mendrisio it's only a short distance to Como, and the end of the trip.

Route 3b: Lugano to Menaggio

Lugano – Gandria –Porlezza – Menaggio (28km/17 miles) *See map, p29*

This route leads from Lugano via the very picturesque village of Gandria to Menaggio on Lake Como. The route goes through regions that are not only very scenic but have also produced several fine artists and architects over the centuries.

Leave Lugano along the road to Porlezza, which follows a steep section beyond Castagnola with fine views across the lake and the Sighignola Massif. Along this section of road it's actually quite easy to miss ★ **Gandria**, which

Gandria promenade

s just below the route. This much-visited village is a
mble of houses on a steep slope right beside the lake,
d is very picturesque, especially when viewed from
e water. It can be reached on foot from Castagnola (1hr)
ong a path lined with subtropical vegetation. On the
posite bank is the Cantine di Gandria landing stage. Here
e original **Museo Doganale** or Customs Museum (Easter
mid-October daily 1.30–5.30pm), is worth a brief visit;
contains a fascinating selection of smuggled goods of
kinds.

eyond Gandria the route crosses the Italian border. The
mlet of San Mamete marks the entrance to the pic-
resque ★ **Valsolda**, a long valley surrounded by high
olomite peaks which is very popular with hikers and
mbers. The small village of **Puria** was the birthplace of
e most important artist-architect of the Lombard Re-
issance, Pellegrino Tibaldi (1527–96). He worked in
s region and also in Rome and Milan, but his career took
f properly when he worked for Philip II in Madrid. Val-
lda was also the home of the Italian author Antonio
gazzaro (1842–1911), whose novel *Piccolo Mondo An-
o* is set in this region. The majestic mountains and the
ke provide an atmospheric backdrop for the ★ **Santu-
io della Madonna della Caravina**, a magnificent
roque structure built in 1663, and situated above the
in road between Cressogno and Cima.

e town of **Porlezza** (pop. 3,800) marks the eastern end
Lake Lugano. It dates back to prehistoric times, and
ring the Roman era was the port of *Raetia*. Later on this
hing town, like so many others between Lakes Mag-
ore and Como, was the home of several generations of
ists, including the Sanmichele and Della Porta families.
glielmo della Porta was a pupil of Michelangelo, and
famous for his work on the dome of St Peter's in Rome
ter his master's death in 1564. Unfortunately Porlezza
s no important artistic monuments of its own. The parish
urch of **San Vittore** (17th-century with fresco deco-
tion) is worth a visit, as is the Romanesque campanile
the ruined church of San Maurizio, far outside the town
the foot of the Monte Calbiga (1,698m/5,570ft). The
urch marks the site of the former Porlezza, which was
stroyed in a landslide. Remains of an early medieval set-
ment were discovered during archaeological excava-
ns in the area.

ere are several good excursions from Porlezza. Try vis-
ng **Osteno** on the southern shore of Lake Lugano, with
attractive church; inside there is an astounding mar-
e ★ *Madonna and Child* by Andrea Bregno, dated 1464.

A fine backdrop…

33

…and perfect views

Halfway between Porlezza and Osteno the road leads pa[st] the entrance to the **Grotte di Rescia**, a small limesto[ne] cavern.

Not far away from Porlezza is the ★ **Val Cavargna**[,] picturesque mountain region with several pretty village[s,] magnificent chestnut groves and beech forests, a pro[fu]sion of wild flowers and numerous walking and hiki[ng] routes. One well-surfaced route connects Porlezza wi[th] both the Val Cavargna and the **Val Rezzo**, and a 30-k[m] (18-mile) round trip by car affords several magnifice[nt] views of the region. Note the abandoned mountain ha[m]lets, however: the problem of depopulation is affecti[ng] many of these Southern Alpine valleys.

Several more marked routes lead from Buggio[lo] (1,035m/3,400ft) to the Passo di San Lucio (1,548[m/] 5,050ft; 2hrs), an ancient way of gaining access to t[he] Val Colla in Ticino, and along the ridge of the Mo[nte] Garzirola (2,116m/6,940ft; 2hrs from San Lucio), whi[ch] is famed for its magnificent panoramic views.

The road to Menaggio leads past the small and shallo[w] Lago di Piano, which has a maximum depth of around 5[m] (16ft) and was once a part of Lake Lugano. Toweri[ng] above the vineyards of Carlazzo here is the high roc[ky] peak of **Monte Grona** (1,736m/5,695ft), and across to t[he] right is the forest-covered northern flank of **Mo[nte] Tremezzo** (1,700m/5,570ft).

At the tiny hamlet of Croce, the road begins its win[d]ing descent to the western bank of Lake Como, with so[me] good views of Ballagio and the mountains around the V[al]sassina. One particularly good view of the lake and [its] mountain backdrop can be enjoyed from the **Crocetta [di] Specchi** (505m/1,650ft), easily and quickly reached fr[om] Croce; it takes around an hour to climb the Sasso di S[an] Martino (862m/2,820ft), where a magnificent panora[ma] meets the eye, extending northeast as far as the gran[ite] peaks of the Bergell.

The town of **Menaggio** (pop. 3,200) lies on a sm[all] promontory at the point where the Val Sanagra meets La[ke] Como. This is also where the important connecting ro[ad] with Lugano branches off, resulting in chaotic traffic co[n]ditions (particularly in the summer). The area slightly i[n]land, with its hiking routes and excursion destinatio[ns,] is far more peaceful and attractive. A winding road lea[ds] north to Plesio and on to **Breglia**, with its little Mado[nna] di Breglia church, visible from afar, and also the obse[r]vation point known as the Belvedere San Domeni[co] (820m/2,690ft). From Breglia, hikers can follow the p[ath] to the **Rifugio Menaggio** (superb views of Lake Co[mo)] and from there continue to the summit of Monte Gro[na]

Passing glance

Menaggio fishmonger

omo

e city of ★★ **Como** (pop. 95,000) has two distinct faces:
e noble one, facing the lake, and the ugly one that ex-
nds into the Brianza. The best direction to approach
omo from is north, either across the lake or along one
the lakeside roads. This is when the town is at its most
agical: green, grey and a soft ochre, bathed in Mediter-
nean light, the walls of the old town retain a sobriety that
distinctly Lombard. From this angle it's impossible to
e behind the noble facade and into Como's industrial
art. The first craftsmen to make the town famous were
e architects and stonemasons from the region, known as
aestri Comacini, who built such magnificent Lombard
chitecture; and the town's industrial future was secured
the introduction of silk manufacturing in 1510 by Pietro
oldoni. *Pura seta di Como* is a phrase often heard in-
rnationally nowadays, and the silk industry of this re-
on accounts for almost one quarter of world production:
ery day Como produces the equivalent of 250km (155
iles) of silk ribbon!

Como Cathedral: carving detail

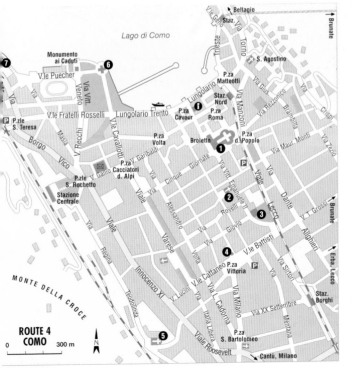

ROUTE 4
COMO
0   300 m

History

Growing up in Como

Though inhabited long before the Romans arrived, Como is most famous historically as the birthplace of Pliny the Elder (AD24–79), compiler of the 37-volume *Natural Historia*, and of his nephew Pliny the Younger (AD62–113). The Romans were followed by Lombards and Franks, and during the Middle Ages Como suffered from several battles between the Guelphs (pro-papacy) and the Ghibellines (pro-empire). During the Ten Years' War with Milan (1118–27) the town was partially destroyed but managed to recover largely because of support from the emperor Barbarossa. From 1335 Como was ruled by the Visconti, and from 1450 by the Sforza, and flourished culturally as a result – in contrast to Spanish rule, which lasted until 1714. Economic recovery only really began under the Austrian Habsburgs, and the silk industry in particular made Como quite prosperous again. Today the old town of Como – the *città murata* – is largely closed to motor traffic, and its layout is almost identical to that of the original Roman *castrum* on the site. For some time now there has been a complete ban on new construction; restoration is the order of the day. Como's ancient walls and arcades are ideal for a stroll back into the centuries, and the gourmet specialities and exclusive fashions make shopping here a very memorable experience.

Cathedral interior

City Tour

The best place to start a tour of the historic old town is the cathedral square, in which the ★★ **Cathedral ❶**, the **Broletto** (former town hall, built in 1215) and the **Torre del Comune** (old city tower) make up a harmonious and grandiose architectural ensemble. Both the Torre del Comune and the Broletto, with its Tuscan-style black-and

Refreshment on the piazza

white patterned facade, date from the early 13th century; the cathedral was begun somewhat later, in 1396, and construction work continued – with the odd interruption – right into the 18th century. The 75-m (245-ft) high dome above the crossing, for instance, was built in 1744 by the Turin architect Juvara. Nevertheless, the building as a whole is exceptionally harmonious. Lorenzo degli Spagli's original design was Gothic; the ★ facade, begun in 1457, is considered a masterpiece of Early Lombard Renaissance architecture. Much of its statuary is by the Rodari brothers, e.g. the *Adoration of the Magi* relief in the lunette, and the two seated figures placed proudly on either side of the main portal, Pliny the Elder and Pliny the Younger. Tommaso and Jacopo Rodari also did the so-called Porta della Rana or 'Frog Portal' on the northern side of the cathedral, which owes its name to a rather sketchy relief of a frog.

Looking towards the altar

The interior of the cathedral is rather dark, but it contains several artistic masterpieces including the enormous 16th-century Tuscan and Flemish tapestries lining the nave, a fine *Deposition* by Tommaso Rodari in the left transept, and several altar paintings by the great Bernardino Luini (*Adoration of the Magi*) and also Gaudenzio Ferrari (*Flight from Egypt*).

37

Just a few short steps away from the cathedral is the church of ★ **San Fedele** ❷, a Romanesque basilica built above the ruins of a previous Carolingian structure on the site during the 12th century. The apse with its dwarf gallery and the trefoil ground-plan are both reminiscent of Charlemagne's Palatine Chapel in Aachen. The northern portal has some very fine sculpture work, and inside to the left of the northern apse there are several frescoes dating from the 12th and 13th centuries, thematically related to the ones in the baptistery of Riva San Vitale (*see page 31*).

Museum vase

The Palazzo Giovio houses the ★ **Museo Archeologico Artistico** ❸ (Tuesday to Saturday 9.30am–12.30pm and 2–5pm, Sunday 10am–1pm), one of Como's two municipal museums. The oldest finds here date from around 1000BC, and there are also several fascinating Roman, Romanesque and Gothic exhibits. The **picture gallery** documents Lombard art of the 16th to 18th centuries, and there is also an exotic section displaying art from the various Mediterranean cultures. The other museum, the **Museo del Risorgimento G Garibaldi** (Tuesday to Saturday 9.30am–12.30pm and 2–5pm, Sunday 10am–1pm), inside the neoclassical Palazzo Olginati next door to the Palazzo Giovio, has some interesting exhibits documenting the town's history, its 19th-century liberation struggles and the two World Wars.

Lombard painting in the gallery

Family outing

One of the most majestic gates still surviving from Como's medieval fortifications is the mighty **Torre di Porta Vittoria ❹**, a full 40m (130ft) high, with its over-sized double windows. From the Piazza Vittoria it's not far to the church of ★★ **Sant'Abbondio ❺** which, despite its location between the railway line and some ugly industrial buildings, is one of the most important Early Lombard Romanesque structures in Italy. The five-aisled basilica with its two bell-towers has several stylistic features in common with structures north of the Alps (e.g. Speyer Cathedral in Germany). The strikingly large choir contains Gothic frescoes dating from around 1350, and the ★ cloister to the north of the building, with its twin-storeyed arcade, was added in the 16th century.

Tempting cakes in Como

There's a good view of the town and the lake from the **Castello Baradello** (access via the Piazza San Rocco), a picturesque ruined fort on the eastern slopes of the Monte della Croce (536m/1,760ft). Out on the western side of the harbour is the neoclassical structure known as the **Tempio Voltano ❻** (daily except Monday 10am–noon and 3–6pm, October to March 2–4pm), dedicated to the famous physicist and discoverer Alessandro Volta (1745–1827), after whom the electrical unit *volt* is named; his personal effects and also the batteries he invented are on display here.

Youth Hostel at Villa dell'Olmo

The western lake promenade leads from the Piazza Cavour past several attractive neoclassical villas to the ★ **Villa dell'Olmo ❼**, a magnificent estate laid out between 1782 and 1787. Its first important visitor was Napoleon, who arrived here just after the building was completed with his wife Josephine. The Villa dell'Olmo is by far the most majestic of the neoclassical villas in this part of Como.

Route 5

Lake Como

Over the centuries the splendid countryside around Lake Como has been gradually made even more attractive by the hand of man, and it is probably true to say that this lake, known to the Romans as *Lacus Lario*, is the most impressive of the Upper Italian lakes. Not only Como Cathedral but also the rows of magnificent villas with beautiful gardens along the edge of the lake all testify to the wonderfully harmonious blend of natural scenery and architecture in this part of the world. Like a fjord, Lake Como is surrounded by steep mountains. Unlike Lake Maggiore

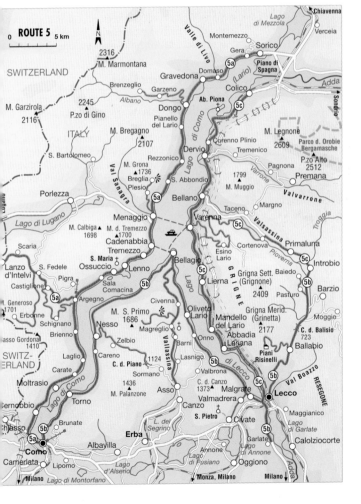

it does not extend across a plain; it is an Alpine lake, de
spite its Mediterranean vegetation, and southern-baroqu
style villas and parks. But this contrast is what makes th
Lario, as it is called locally, so attractive. Even though
surface area of 146sq km (56sq miles) makes it only th
third-largest lake in Upper Italy, with its depth of 410r
(1,350ft) it is the deepest inland lake in Europe. Lak
Como is roughly 50km (32 miles) long and 4.5km (
miles) across at its widest point. It is unusually-shaped
reminding most people of an upside-down 'Y'. The mai
rivers flowing into the lake are the Mera, which descend
from the Bergell, and the Adda, which has its source in th
Bernina Massif, leaves the lake near Lecco and finall
joins the Po not far from Cremona.

The high, rocky peaks to the east of Lake Como certainl
provide the most impressive view, but the western shore
too, has several delights of its own a little further inlanc

5a – The Western Shore

**Cernobbio – Tremezzo – Menaggio – Gravedona
Sorico (59km/37 miles)** *See map, p39*

The route up the lake from Como first arrives at **Cer
nobbio** (pop. 8,000), where the **Villa d'Este** begins th
long line of famous residences along the lake's wester
shore. Built between 1565–70 by Pellegrino Tibaldi, th
villa was altered in the early 19th century by Caroline c
Brunswick in accordance with contemporary taste. Toda
the Villa d'Este is a luxury hotel and open only to guest

Guests at the Villa d'Este

Pass the magnificent gardens and villas to reach **Carat**
where the small 11th-century church of Santa Maria is jus
A sedate form of recreation a short distance above the main road. The Romanesqu

ampanile, 15th-century frescoes and fine view of the lake
ll form a very memorable ensemble.

The small town of **Argegno** is a good starting-point for
detour into the ★ **Intelvi Valley**, a high plateau with some
elightful landscape, but famed above all for producing
whole host of painters, architects and stonemasons.
hese *Maestri Antelami* not only influenced Lombard
rt for decades but were active all over Europe and even
ie Near East. Several of these masters have also left traces
ere in the Valle d'Intelvi: in **Scaria**, for instance, which
as superb stucco work by Diego Carlone and frescoes by
arlo Carlone. Keep your eyes open in this valley – there
re several artistic and architectural discoveries to be made.
he Valle d'Intelvi is a paradise for nature-lovers too, how-
ver; its unique location between Lake Lugano and Lake
omo provides a whole series of magnificent panoramic
iews to accompany hikes. One particularly impressive
eak for climbers to head for here is the **Sassa Gordona**
l,410m/4,625ft).

Uphill struggle in the Intelvi Valley

Scaria parish church

ist before Sala Comacina, the only island in Lake Como
omes into view, the **Isola Comacina**. Around 600m
40yds) long and up to 200m (220yds) wide, the island
as more important historically than it is today. It was set-
ed during Roman times, and during the Middle Ages
ere were five churches on it at one point. In 1169 the set-
ement on the island was wiped out by Como in retalia-
on for its pact with Milan during the Ten Years' War
118–27). All that remains today of the original town
re the ruined walls of the Romanesque basilica of
ant'Eufemia.

41

Isola Comacina: coffee ceremony

Ossuccio fisherman

t the entrance to the Val Perlana is **Ossuccio** (pop. 1,500),
here the simple church of Santa Maria Maddalena has
i unusual campanile with a brick belfry, dating from
e 14th century. Above the village is a 17th-century Via
rucis with 14 chapels, and higher still, the basilica of
San Benedetto in the Val Perlana is probably the finest
f the Romanesque churches on the lake. **Lenno** also has
i interesting church: **Santo Stefano**, though much ren-
vated during the 16th century, is originally Lombard. The
ypt was part of an 11th-century basilica, and remains
a Roman bath have been discovered beneath the church.
into Stefano's octagonal baptistery also dates from the
I th century.

irther along the route, **Mezzegra** comes into view. The
ace is famous for one reason: it was here on 28 April
)45, one day after having been taken prisoner in nearby
ongo while trying to flee to Switzerland, that Benito
Iussolini and his mistress Clara Petacci were shot dead.

Villa Carlotta

The two resorts of ★ **Tremezzo** (pop. 1,300) and **Cadenabbia** are almost always busy, especially in the area round the ★★★ **Villa Carlotta** (daily March to October), the most famous and the most lavishly decorative villa on Lake Como. Innumerable visitors come here each year to marvel at the magnificent ★ terraced garden, the elegant rooms (e.g. the great marble hall), the sculpture and painting collection (including works by Canova and Thorvaldsen) and the fine view across the lake to the Bellagio peninsula and the grey rocks of the Grigna. The Villa Carlotta was originally built in the baroque style (1747) and received its present neoclassical appearance at the beginning of the 19th century. It was sold to Princess Marie of Prussia in 1856, and she bequeathed it to her daughter Charlotte. No trip to the Lake Como region is complete without a visit to this superb building.

The route now continues on to **Menaggio** (*see Route 3, page 34*), beyond which the landscape gradually begins to get starker, and generally more Alpine than Mediterranean. Snowy mountain peaks start appearing; the northern end of the *Lario* is only around 40km (24 miles) away from the main Alpine range. The lakeshore road leads through Sant'Abbondio, Rezzonico and the collection of communities making up Pianello del Lario. There's a good ★ **boat museum** (daily July to mid-September) in the community of Calozzo, where many of the various boat types used on the lakes are exhibited, including gondolas, fishing boats and punts.

Gravedona: Palazzo Gallio

The historic centre of the upper part of Lake Como is ★ **Gravedona** (pop. 3,000), an independent commune during medieval times which later became famous for its goldsmiths. Right next to the lake is the **Palazzo Gallio**, built in 1583 according to designs by Pellegrino Tibaldi, on the site of a ruined fort that was destroyed during the Milan-Como war of 1118–27. Don't miss the church of ★ **Santa Maria del Tiglio** on the south side of the town: it is one of the most important Romanesque churches on Lake Como, and was originally an Early Christian baptistery (remains of mosaics and font). The facade is dominated by the tall, octagonal tower, and inside, a monumental 13th-century statue of Christ opens his arms in welcome. The neighbouring church of San Vicenzo dates from the 11th century, but was altered completely (apart from the crypt) during the 17th and 18th centuries.

Gravedona is dominated by the church of **Santa Maria delle Grazie**, built in 1467 as part of an Augustinian monastery. It contains important frescoes by 15th- and 16th-century Lombard artists. A word of warning, though: the place is hardly ever open!

b – Como to Lecco via Bellagio

'omo – Bellagio – Lecco (52km/32 miles) *See map, p39*

See map, p39

he trips to Bellagio, the 'Pearl of the Lake', and to Lecco
'e both breathtaking, and if you combine them with de-
·urs into the higher regions between the two arms of the
ke – Monte San Primo, for instance (1,686m/5,530ft),
· at least the Madonna del Ghisallo observation point
'55m/2,450ft), the experience is unforgettable. The best
ews are of course to be had at Bellagio, the most famous
sort on the lake; it is uniquely situated and still has an
1mistakeable charm of its own, even in these days of
eavy traffic and mass tourism. Approaching Bellagio
y steamer from Como is an unforgettable experience. The
1ads along the lakeshore are very quiet in contrast, and
at's not only because of all their hairpins. The villages
ong the steep shores are sleepy and picturesque, set
;ainst the blue backdrop of the lake, and there are far
ore old buildings than new ones. To really enjoy this
1te, allow two days and spend the night in Bellagio;
ose with less time will have to make do with one day.

1ere are several villas between Como and **Torno** , among
em the magnificent ★ **Pliniana** – which, by the way, has
·thing to do with either Pliny the Elder or the Younger.
1e Pliniana was built in 1575 by Pellegrino Tibaldi, the
chitect who designed the villa for Como's governor Gio-
nni Anguissola. History books mention the count's in-
·lvement in the murder of Duke Pier Luigi Farnese (a
n of Pope Paul III and one of the most evil men of the
:naissance). The villa had several changes of owner af-
· that, but also many illustrious guests, including Byron,
endhal, Napoleon, Liszt and Rossini – who wrote his
era *Tancredi* here in just six days. The villa is not open
the public.

Torno

The route to Bellagio: Nesso

Boating on a blue lake

*Bellagio bathers and
the approach to Villa Melzi*

The old part of Torno has several picturesque corners. The church of **San Giovanni** is Romanesque in origin (12th-century campanile), and was extended in the 15th century. Note the Early Christian tombstone in the nave.

The views get better and better as you continue towards Bellagio. One very pretty village is Careno, part of the municipality of **Nesso** (pop. 1,700), where the houses almost seem to be above rather than next to each other. Above Careno is the entrance to the **Grotta Masera**, one of several caverns in this region. Up on the **Colma del Piano** (1,124m/3,687ft), 12km (7 miles) from Nesso, there is a magnificent view across the valleys and mountains surrounding Asso and Canzo.

The town of ★★★ **Bellagio** (pop. 4,000) really lives up to its name. Its dramatic location at the point where Lake Como and Lake Lecco divide combines with the panorama, the villas and the gardens to produce a truly admirable work of man. The Romans called it *Bilacus* ('between the lakes'). The promontory is approached in real style by ship, and it becomes clear why Flaubert wrote *on voudrait vivre ici et y mourir* when he first caught sight of Bellagio.

The tiny Borgo lies on the western side of the narrow peninsula. Narrow flights of steps lead up from the lake promenade to the parish church of **San Giacomo**. This three-aisled Romanesque structure with its 17th-century tower contains a very expressive *Entombment* attributed to Perugino (c. 1500).

But what would Bellagio be without its villas and its ★★ parks? Some of them have a very varied history, such as the one surrounding the **Villa Giulia** on the eastern side of the peninsula, formerly the residence of Belgian king

eopold I and today in private hands. On the hill above
[t]e town is the ★ **Villa Serbelloni** (guided tours daily
[1]0am–4pm), originally Renaissance but with neoclassi-
[c]al additions. One of the two villas owned by Pliny the
[Y]ounger formerly stood on this site; later on it was con-
[v]erted into a Lombard fortress.

The entrance to the second large park in Ballagio, the
[o]ne surrounding the ★ **Villa Melzi**, is in the suburb of Lop-
[p]ia on the road to Como. The cool, neoclassical villa was
[b]uilt in 1815, and the park (9am–6pm), dotted with stat-
[u]es, has a marvellous collection of exotic plants (avenues
[o]f plane trees, azaleas, alpine roses). Another very ro-
[m]antic place is the **Buco dei Carpi**, a cavern down by

Azaleas line the waterfront

[th]e lake 5km (3 miles) out of Bellagio in the direction of
[C]omo, with very attractive light effects reminiscent of the
[B]lue Grotto on Capri.

Alongside its villas and parks Bellagio also has moun-
[ta]ins, and the somewhat steep and rocky hinterland is ideal
[fo]r hikes and excursions. Try a drive up to the **Madonna**
[d]el Ghisallo (755m/2,477ft) via **Civenna**, a delightful re-
[so]rt above the eastern arm of the Lario. The best place
[fo]r a view in the triangle formed by Como, Lecco and Bel-
[la]gio (Traigola Lariano) is the ★ **Monte San Primo**
[(1],686m/5,530ft), which offers a breathtaking panorama.
[T]he path to the summit can be reached by driving south
[fr]om Bellagio and turning right in Guello.

45

[C]ontinue onwards now via Malgrate to reach **Lecco** (pop.
[4]4,000), with its smoking factory chimneys and traffic
[ch]aos. Very little remains of its former beauty these days.
[N]evertheless, Lecco is definitely worth a visit, not least
[be]cause it is the setting of one of the most famous books
[in] the world: *I promessi sposi* (*The Betrothed*) by Italy's
[gr]eatest Romantic novelist, Alessandro Manzoni (1785–
[18]73). Written in 1827, the book had immense patriotic
[ap]peal for Italians of the nationalistic Risorgimento pe-
[ri]od, and is a sympathetic portrayal of the struggle of two
[pe]asant lovers to marry in the face of opposition from a
[vi]cious local landowner and the local parish priest.

Manzoni in Lecco

[L]ecco has several interesting sights. At the southwest-
[er]n corner of the central square is the battlemented **Torre**
[de]l Castello, part of a former 15th-century Visconti
[fo]rtress, and housing the **Museo del Risorgimento e della**
[R]esistenza. The nearby **Ponte Azzone Visconti** also dates
[ba]ck to the days of the Visconti (1336–38). In the sub-
[ur]b of Caleotti, the 18th-century neoclassical **Villa Man-**
[zo]ni is where the famous author (*see above*) spent his
[yo]uth. The 18th-century **Palazzo Belgioioso** contains the
[N]atural History Museum, which has several fascinating
[pr]ehistoric and Roman exhibits from the region, includ-
[in]g a valuable relief dating from the 1st century BC.

Palazzo Belgioioso

Lecco's impressive surroundings

Culture vulture

Lecco is indisputably ugly, but the scenery surrounding it is not. The lake and the mountains are quite magnificent, and ideal for excursions. One hour's walk away from the village of **Civate** is the church of ★★ **San Pietro al Monte** (639m/2,100ft). Why a Benedictine monastery was founded here in this remote mountain region during the 8th century is not known, but the architecture blends in very harmoniously with the scenery. Originally San Pietro was a hall church with an eastern apse; during the 11th century the entrance was switched to the eastern end to create direct access to the Oratorio San Benedetto, a centralised Romanesque structure situated further down. San Pietro's main claim to fame is its stucco and frescoes dating from the late 11th century, revealing the influence of Byzantine artists. The lunette fresco showing angels fighting a seven-headed dragon is very fine, as is the stucco work on the baldachin. The crypt contains further reliefs and frescoes.

★ The **Grigna** is the vast limestone massif next to Lecco, between the eastern shore of Lake Como and the Valsassina, and its highest points are the Grignon (2,409m/7,900ft) and the Grignetta (2,177m/7,140ft) both of them with a vast choice of hiking possibilities. The southern Grigna is particularly reminiscent of the Dolomites; an interesting 3-hr route – for experienced climbers only – connects it with the Grignone.

5c – The Eastern Shore

Lecco – Lierna – Varenna – Colico (41km/25 miles) See map, p39

The stretch along the eastern shore of Lake Como can easily be covered in half an hour, thanks to the new highway. Although the trip does give an idea of the sheer length of this relic from the Ice Age, lying like an 'Alpine fjord' between its steep shores, to get to know the lake and its hinterland allow one day to follow this route

The first town on the eastern shore of the Lago di Lecco – the name given to the eastern arm of Lake Como – **Abbadia Lariana** (pop. 2,200), 7km (4 miles) outside Lecco. The name refers to a long-vanished Benedictine monastery; the oldest traces of settlement date back to pre Roman times. Most of the older buildings can be found in the upper part of the town, and there's a good view from the **Monte di Borbino** (486m/1,600ft), a 30-min walk from the town centre. Abbadia Lariana's old silk factory, built in 1919, has now been turned into a small museum; the highlight here is an enormous water-driven silk-spinning machine with 432 bobbins.

The main reason the town of **Mandello del Lario** (pop. ,500) became famous is because of motor bikes – produced by the firm of Guzzi (founded in 1921). The bikes ave been successful for decades in races all over the vorld. Apart from all that horsepower, Mandello also has everal cultural-historical attractions: the parish church of **San Lorenzo** (9th, 12th and 17th-century), several old araded townhouses and also the richly-decorated church of **Madonna del Fiume**, one of the most successful baroque uildings in the region. The smaller, 15th-century church of **San Nicolò** has a number of interesting late medieval eatures, both inside and out.

Further on, **Lierna** (pop. 1,500) is a very old area of settlement: finds dating from the Bronze Age and the foundations of a Roman villa have been discovered here. The small church in the suburb of Castello used to be part of a medieval castle. It's worth stopping briefly to admire the shortest river in Italy: the Fiumelatte, or 'milk stream', just outside Varenna. From its source to the lake it covers a total distance of 250m (820ft), and this earned it a mention in Leonardo da Vinci's *Codice Atlantico*. Because of a geological phenomenon, its milky waters only flow between spring and autumn.

Vertigo in Varenna

47

At the widest part of the lake (4.5km/3 miles) lies the small town of ★ **Varenna** (pop. 1,000), with its picturesque centre of piled-up houses intersected by narrow alleys and dominated by the tower of the parish church of San Giorgio. The basilica dates from around 1300, but underwent several alterations in the 17th and 18th centuries. There is a noteworthy *Baptism of Christ* (1553) altar painting here by Sigismondo de Magistris. Just outside the town is the **Villa Monastero** (April to October 9.30am–noon

Villa Monastero: the grounds

Villa Monastero: detail

Valsassina Valley

Striving for perfection

and 2.30–6pm) with its magnificent grounds. The buildin was originally a convent, founded by the Cistercians i 1208 for nuns who had been evicted from Isola Comacin and dissolved in 1567 because of the reputation of promi cuity gained by their successors. After several chang of ownership the villa is now a science centre owned b the Italian state.

Don't miss a detour from Varenna to ★ **Esino Lario** (po 800). Situated at the top of a steep and winding road, th small town of many villas is sometimes known as th 'Pearl of the Grigna'. From the parish church there's a vie westwards as far as Lake Lugano, and the peaks of th Grigna can be seen to the southeast. The **Museo del Grigna** contains some fascinating local finds (July an August daily 9am–noon and 4–7pm). Another excursio from Varenna goes via the 'Panoramica del Lario', an leads into the **Valsassina**, a magnificent southern Alpin valley much favoured by the Ancient Romans.

Continue now to **Bellano** (pop. 4,500). The 14th-centur black-and-white striped facade and rose window of th parish church of SS Nazaro e Celso are worthy of not but the real tourist attraction here is the *orrido*, a wild romantic and very steep gorge (only recommended f those with a head for heights) just outside the town.

Not far away from the relatively uninteresting industri town of **Dervio** (pop. 2,400) is the picturesque little vi lage of ★ **Corenno Plinio**, which is said to derive its nam from its early settlers who came from Corinth and fro Pliny the Elder who gave the site his highest praise. Th village church, ruined fortifications and pretty old hous are all huddled together attractively on a small rise next the lake.

A bit further along, romantically situated on a peni sula, is ★ **Piona Abbey**. It was founded as long ago the 7th century, but the existing buildings are of far lat origin: San Nicolò was consecrated in 1138, and its ma nificent cloister dates from the 13th century. Today th abbey is occupied by Cistercians who not only lead an e emplary life on their idyllic island but also produce a d licious liqueur.

The northernmost town on the eastern shore of Lake Con is **Colico** (pop. 5,000). The rough mountains round abo lend it an almost Alpine appearance, and the ruins of th old fortress up on the **Montecchio** to the northeast of Co ico blend in with the landscape. Originally built by th Spanish at the beginning of the 17th century, the fortre was destroyed in 1798 by the French.

Route 6

Bergamo

Bergamo, known as *Bergomum* to the Romans, consists of two sections: the 'upper town' *(alta)*, which is the oldest part, and the more modern lower section *(bassa* or *piana)*. It was originally a settlement of the Celtic tribe of the *Orobi*, but became a Roman town in 196BC. After its destruction at the hands of Attila the Hun it became the seat of a Lombard duchy, and by the 12th century the town had become an independent commune. From 1329 onwards the Visconti family ruled, but in 1428 it became Venetian property, remaining so until 1797 when the French took control and included it in Napoleon's Cisalpine Republic. Bergamo owes much of its architectural and artistic beauty to the long years of Venetian rule. In 1815 the city became Austrian, and remained so until 1859 when it became part of the Kingdom of Italy.

Palazzo della Ragione

City Tour

The two parts of the city are linked by a rack railway. The older, upper part is closed to traffic, and the best place to begin a stroll through is the **Piazza Vecchia** ❶. Note the Venetian lions on the **Contarini Fountain** in the middle, erected in 1780 during the final years of Venetian rule by Mayor Contarini. It's worth going up the Torre del Comune for a very rewarding view. Continue now from the Piazza Vecchia to the Piazza del Duomo, or Cathedral Square. Bergamo's Romanesque cathedral was rebuilt

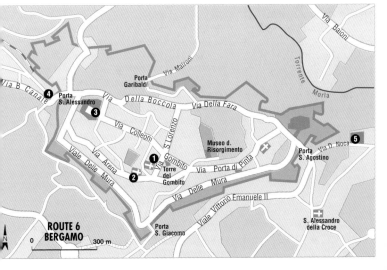

ROUTE 6
BERGAMO
0   300 m

Santa Maria Maggiore

Colleoni Chapel

Donizetti remembered

in 1483 and 1639; its white facade is almost complete hidden from view by the buildings surrounding it. Despi its simple beauty, the Duomo is however completely u staged by the adjacent 12th-century basilica of ★ **San** **Maria Maggiore** ❷, begun in 1137 and rebuilt durir the 14th and 15th centuries. The red-and-white marb porch dates from the 13th century, and highlights insi the church include not only several magnificent 16th-ce tury Flemish and Florentine tapestries but also the tom of Bergamo's most famous son, the operatic compos Gaetano Donizetti (1797–1848). Donizetti wrote over 2 operas in his lifetime, and the most famous are probab *Lucia di Lammermoor* and *Don Pasquale*. Considered t king of Italian opera for many years, he was eventual eclipsed by Verdi. Lovers of architecture come to th church from all over the world to admire the ★★★ **Colleo** **Chapel**, a Renaissance masterpiece built between 147 and 1476 by Giovanni Antonio Amadeo, with ceiling fre coes by Tiepolo. Colleoni was a notorious *condottie* (mercenary) who fought on several different sides du ing his successful military career, earning enough in th process to have himself suitably immortalised (his eque trian statue can be admired in front of the Scuola S Marco in Venice). Don't leave the Piazza del Duomo wit out first admiring the polygonal **baptistery**, built in 134 it used to stand inside Santa Maria Maggiore.

Stroll westwards now as far as the Piazza Cittadell where you will find the 13th-century **Citadel** ❸ whic today houses a museum of geology and natural histor with several fascinating exhibits. The Torre dei Adalber in this square was built in the 13th century, and is al known as the 'Tower of Hunger'. Just behind the Citade on the other side of the city gate known as the Porta Sar Alessandro, is the **Donizetti Birthplace Museum** ❹ No 14, Borgo Canale.

Walk back across the upper town to the Piazza Vecchi and from there continue eastwards as far as Bergamo's cu tural highlight *par excellence*, the ★★ **Accademia Ca** **rara** ❺. This art gallery, founded in the 18th century b Count Giacomo Carrara to house his collection of pain ings, contains several superb works by artists such as T ian, Raphael, Botticelli, Velasquez and Mategna – to nan but a few. Allow plenty of time for any visit here!

Bergamo's 'lower town' also has several attractions i cluding the church of **San Bartolomeo**, with its larg ★ altarpiece by the Late Renaissance artist Lorenzo Lot (1480–1556). Lotto was famous for his perceptive po traits and mystical paintings of religious subjects. He liv in Bergamo from 1513 onwards, and it was here that h style matured.

ake Iseo *See map, p52–3*

ake Iseo, situated between Bergamo and Brescia, lies 6m (610ft) above sea level, is 25km (15 miles) long, has maximum width of 5km (3 miles), a maximum depth 250m (820ft), and a surface area of 62sq km (24sq les). Named *Sebinus Lacus* by the Romans, it is the sev- th-largest lake in Italy.

his route goes around the lake in a clockwise direction, arting at the small town of **Sarnico**, which already pro- des a foretaste of the natural scenery in store. The moun- ins along the western shore descend steeply towards e lake, while the area of reeds across to the east is framed rolling meadows full of flowers. The uniformity of e landscape is interrupted by the odd colourful camp- e, and small sailing boats can often be seen on the dark- een water.

Sarnico

51

Olive groves, vineyards and avenues of cypress trees e the road, which goes through a series of illuminated nnels. The steep shore between Tavernola and Riva di lto is unspoilt. Venice quarried the black marble for San arco here, and for many years this region was only ac- ssible by boat; the road here was only completed in 1910. Soon the main town on Lake Iseo comes into view: overe. This cheerful community has few old buildings, t to make up for that there is an astonishingly good llection of paintings and porcelain at the **Museo Tadini** aster to October daily 3–6pm, Sunday and public hol- ays 10am–noon). Don't miss the coffee and cake here ther – it's absolutely delicious and also far cheaper than many other places.

Local souvenirs

Life on the water

The eastern shore starts off promisingly, but roman[ce] tends to dissipate after the first few miles. The old ro[ad] winds pleasantly past several old villas along the sho[re] as far as Pisogne, but then suddenly widens to accom[mo]date heavy goods traffic. Don't rush at this point, oth[er]wise you'll miss the 15th-century Augustinian churc[h] of ★ **Madonna della Neve**, which contains some excel[len]t fresco work by the Renaissance artist Romanino.

The next stop is **Sulzano**, picturesquely situated besi[de] a yachting harbour, and the starting-point for ferry tri[ps] (quarter-hourly until 1am) across to the largest island [on] any Italian lake, ★★ **Monte Isola**. This 'island-mountain', 600m (1,970ft) high and covered with thick chestnut fo[r]est and ancient olive groves, is a haven of tranquillit[y]. To ensure that it remains so, only the locals are allowe[d]

Ferry to Monte Isola

use the car ferry. Those reluctant to do the 3-hr walk around the island can travel by shuttle bus between the [v] communities, and there's also a bicycle hire service. [?]e 40-minute ascent from the village of Peschiera [M]araglio to the 16th-century pilgrimage church of **[M]adonna della Ceriola** is well worth it for the superb [?]ew of the sparkling lake below and the two offshore [?]lands of San Paolo and Loreto.

[A] real highlight completes this brief tour of the lake: ★ **Iseo** [?]self. The entrance to it via the 15th-century Castello Old-[?]edi is absolutely delightful. The various narrow alleys [?]eet up at the arcaded Piazza Garibaldi, the town's me-[?]eval market-place with its tiny 14th-century church of **[?]nta Maria del Mercato**. The no less atmospheric

Lakeside houses at Iseo

Bathers and blossoms

Piazza del Sagrato boasts the church of Sant'Andre founded in the 5th century and rebuilt in the 12th, and the right of it is the mausoleum of Giacomo Oldofree who was one of the feudal lords of this region durin medieval times.

One very rewarding car excursion from the Lago d'Ise is to **Capo di Ponte**, halfway up the Val Camonica to t northeast, famed for its ★★ **prehistoric rock engraving** Around 158,000 of these have been discovered, and the date from different periods – some even from Neolith times (8,000 years ago). The engravings, many of whie show hunting scenes and religious symbols, can be a mired in Capo di Ponte's National Rock Engravings Pa *(Parco Nazionale delle Incisioni Rupestri)*, which was d clared a World Heritage Site by UNESCO in 1979.

For another fascinating sight, this time natural rath than man-made, drive inland from the eastern shore ro at Marone and visit the attractive little village of **Zon** Just before the village of Cislano you'll see them: Zone famous ★★ **erosion pillars**. Created by the deposition glacial debris, these fascinating natural columns vary form, and their most unusual features are the boulde perched precariously on top, which make the whole scer even more bizarre.

To the south of Lago d'Iseo, the region of **Franciacor** with its gentle morraine hills is seldom visited by touris but its fine wines and hidden artistic treasures make it fascinating area to explore. From Iseo the most direct li with Lake Garda *(see opposite)* is provided by the ro through Gardone Val Trompia, where the famous Beret guns are manufactured, and on past the cliffs of Nozza ar through Vestone to Lago d'Idro *(see page 70)*.

En route to Capo di Ponte…

…a town with a prehistoric past

Lake Garda

Lake Garda, the largest inland lake in Italy, 51km (31 miles) long and up to 17km (10 miles) wide, is regarded by many as the most beautiful of the Northern Italian lakes. It is 65m (213ft) above sea level. Narrow at its northern end, Lake Garda gradually widens further southwards into a basin that is almost circular, with rich vegetation on its southern and western shores: citrus fruits, laurels, cypresses, vines, oleanders, palm trees and olives all grow here. The lake was referred to as the *Lacus Benacus* by Virgil, Horace and Catullus, but its name changed in the 9th century when the city of Garda was elevated to a county by Charlemagne and acquired dominion over the lake. It is also known as *Benaco*.

Restaurant in Riva

Three Italian provinces border the lake: Trento to the north, Brescia to the west and Verona to the east. This has had a beneficial effect in that each province does its best not to be shown up by the others, and Lake Garda consequently has very well-surfaced roads and also a consistently successful environmental policy ever since the catastrophic pollution of the lake in 1992. The water quality is now acceptable, and a new environmental awareness has taken hold of the entire region.

Lake Garda has an interesting geological history: the glacier that formed it broadened out as it reached the Plain of Lombardy and left a thick layer of moraine. The lake then formed behind this – which explains why the southern part of Lake Garda is relatively shallow in comparison to the deeply gouged northern section (340m/1,110ft). The lake is fed at its northern end by the River Sarca, and at the southern end the River Mincio flows out towards the Po. The entire basin contains 50 million cubic metres of water. There are five islands in Lake Garda, all privately owned: the Isola di Garda (the largest one) in the west measures 9 hectares (22 acres), the Isola San Biagio in the southwest measures only 1 hectare (2½ acres) and the other three – Trimelone, Sogno and dell'Olivo – are so tiny that they don't really merit attention!

Carefree days by the lake

Tourism has had an enormous effect over the past few decades. Lake Garda caters to over 5 million visitors each year, and it's no wonder that the flatter eastern shore is filled with hotels and campsites. The more elegant communities in the north and west are also continuing to expand rapidly and only strict building regulations have managed to halt the construction of faceless apartment blocks and cheap hotels alongside medieval cathedrals. Germans make up the largest contingent of foreign visitors here (62 percent), and when they are joined by the

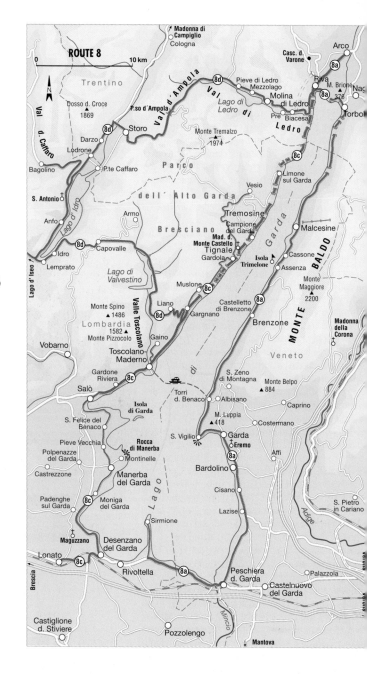

ROUTE 8

0   10 km

56

talians in the summer not one room is available – even he dog kennels are booked out. It's easy to guess the loals' main source of income. Fortunately, however, the reion around the lake has retained its rural character and tructure, and just a few miles inland from the holiday esorts there are vineyards, wheat fields and orchards.

8a – The Eastern Shore

Riva – Malcesine – Torri del Benaco – Garda – Sirmione (75km/47miles)

The scenic stretch of road known as the Gardesana Orintale was completed in 1926, but today has sadly become ne of the most-travelled routes in the region; mile-long queues are an everyday occurrence in peak season, but enerous by-passes are gradually being built to cope with t all. The route is varied from the landscape point of view, eading from Alpine mountains across rolling hills to the road southern plain, and from the surfing paradises of Riva and Torbole past the mighty Monte Baldo massif and he gentle Bardolino wine region to reach the elegant thernal resort of Sirmione at the end of its narrow peninsula. Much of this route can also be covered by bus, and a day sn't really enough to fully appreciate all the contrasts. It's est to cover the eastern shore in stages, not forgetting the elights of 'real Italy' further inland.

The medieval side of Riva

Its turquoise waters

Tradition and elegance are the two most striking characeristics of ★★ **Riva** (pop. 13,000), situated at the northrn end of Lake Garda, where the reflections of the steep oothills of the Alps shimmer in the turquoise water. Riva as long been a favourite of writers and poets. Goethe alled it a 'miracle of nature', and was followed here by tendhal, Kafka, Thomas Mann and DH Lawrence. The own has several interesting sights to offer, and the best lace to begin any stroll is the ★ **Piazza Tre Novembre**, acing out towards the lake and the harbour, and domiated by the steep walls of the Monte Rochetta (1,540m/ ,320ft). The other side of the square is taken up by buildngs in the Venetian-Lombard style with pleasantly cool rcades (14th-century) and the 34-m (111-ft) high **Torre Apponale**; this clock tower was formerly part of the town's ortifications. The 15th-century **Town Hall** (Palazzo Muicipale) is connected by the Porta Bruciata to the 14thentury Palazzo Pretorio, and the coats of arms of the ishops of Trento and Venice can be seen on their facades.

Torre Apponale

From this square the Via Andrea Maffei leads to the Pizza Garibaldi and then to the Piazza Battisti, with the enrance to the ★ **Rocca**, a moated Scaligeri castle complete vith drawbridge. It was built in 1124 and has survived sev-

eral alterations by the Viscontis, the bishops of Trentin and the Venetians. Today it houses the municipal library a concert hall and also the **municipal museum** (Tues day to Saturday 9.30am–5.30pm, Sunday and public hol idays 9.30am–noon and 2–5pm, longer in summer), whic includes a collection of fascinating prehistoric finds fror the pile dwellings at Lake Ledro (*see page* 71).

Another worthwhile sight in Riva is the ★ **Chies dell'Inviolata**, a mighty 18th-century baroque buildin reached via the battlemented San Michele city gate at th end of the Viale Roma. Relatively unadorned on the ou side, this octagonal church has an incredibly orna baroque interior that is well worth a visit.

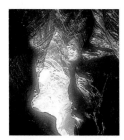

58   *Varone Falls and approach*

There are several good excursions from Riva, includir one to **Arco**, a climbers' paradise. Climbers all descen – or rather ascend – here at the beginning of Septembe each year for the world climbing championships. Arc (pop. 13,800) is 5km (3 miles) north of Lake Garda an is dominated by a 126-m (413-ft) high crag with the ru ins of a medieval fortress on top – the panoramic vie is magnificent. Or why not visit the ★ **Varone Falls**, onl 4km (2 miles) outside Riva? The 'Cascata del Varone' ha been eroding 4mm of rock annually for the past 20,00 years, and the result is a very wild and romantic gorge. Th waterfall can be admired from two grottoes, and warr waterproof clothing is recommended. Another good e: cursion with a magnificent view is to the top of Riva local mountain, the **Monte Brione** (376m/1,230ft), a goc place for hikers and mountain-bikers.

Congregating in Torbole

Further down the lake, **Torbole** is the windsurfing cap tal of the region, and attracts fans of the sport from all ov the world. For non-surfers it isn't the best of places, ar can be rather noisy; wind and weather are of course th main subject of conversation here. The 18th-century pari church of Sant'Andrea contains a noteworthy *Martyrdo of St Matthew* by Giambettino Cignaroli above its alta A short detour from Torbole leads up via the little vi lage of Nago to the so-called ★ **Marmitte dei Gigant** or 'Giants' Pots' – smooth holes in the rock created du ing the last Ice Age by swirling pebbles and meltwater

Malcesine's ancient charm

Now the so-called Riviera degli Olivi begins – the nan refers to the stretch of lakeshore where high alpine scene gently gives way to its Mediterranean equivalent, ar the town of ★★ **Malcesine** (pop. 3,500) comes into vie This former fishing village now lives almost exclusive from tourism, but unlike many other communities Ma cesine has managed to preserve much of its ancient charr The Scaligeri, who ruled this town once like the Viscon

Streets around the castle

before them and the Venetians after them, left a magnificent monument behind: the ★★ **Scaligeri Castle**. Built in the 14th century, this fortress almost cost Goethe his life. Delighted and fascinated by the sight of its mighty battlements, the famous German writer took out his sketch pad – and was immediately placed under arrest on suspicion of being an Austrian spy. Luckily one of the locals recognised his name, and he was released again.

59

Today the panorama from the top of the 33-m (108-ft) high keep can be enjoyed with impunity. It takes only a few minutes to reach the castle along the picturesque alleys of Malcesine, and the place is still remarkably intact, with an upper and a lower section and also three inner courtyards. The former powder room contains a small Goethe exhibition – in memory of the fact that his *Italian Journey* very nearly came to an end here. Several of his sketches can also be admired. The castle also contains the **Museo del Garda e del Baldo** (April to October daily 9am–7pm, November to March weekends only 10am–6pm), containing an exhibition documenting local wildlife.

Down by the harbour

The **Palazzo dei Capitani del Lago** down by the harbour, with its delightful palm garden, was once the seat of the Venetian governors. The entrance hall contains a fresco dated 1672 showing the castle of Malcesine crowned by the Lion of St Mark. The coat of arms of the governors and a fine wooden ceiling can both be admired in the council chamber on the first floor. The highlight of the 18th-century parish church of **Santo Stefano** is a 16th-century *Pietà* by the Veronese artist Girolamo dai Libri.

Excursions from Malcesine include the exciting cable ropeway trip up **Monte Baldo** (daily every 30 minutes 8am–7pm; October and April 9am–6pm, mid-December to March 8am–4.45pm; journey time 10 minutes). The panorama from 1,720m (5,642ft) is quite breathtaking, the restaurants are good, and there's also a botanical garde[n] 1,200m (3,936ft) up the mountain with around 600 di[f]ferent kinds of alpine flower.

Calm waters at Cassone

The Gardesana continues southwards, lined with hotel[s] past several small villages like **Cassone** and **Assenz[a]** as far as **Casteletto**, which is not on the lake but on th[e] other side of the road, on the mountainside. It is a jum[b]le of dark, medieval streets grouped around the Piaz[za] dell'Olivo, with its picturesque houses. South of Caste[l]etto, visit the small 12th-century Romanesque church **San Zeno**, which is something of an architectural rari[ty] with its two aisles and three apses. It was built above R[o]man foundations, and the 15th-century frescoes depict bi[b]lical scenes.

Torri del Benaco: the castle

60

The harbour town of ★ **Torri del Benaco** (pop. 2,600) once again dominated by a 14th-century Scaligeri ca[s]tle, built above the foundations of a 10th-century fort. Th[e] attractively restored castle contains a **museum** (Decem[]ber to March Sunday and public holidays 2.30–5.30p[m], April, May and October daily 9.30am–12.30pm an[d] 2.30–6pm; June to September 9.30am–1pm and 2.30[–]5pm; closed November) documenting everything fro[m] olive cultivation to prehistoric rock drawings. Just sou[th] of the castle is a very old *limonaia*, or lemon garden, whi[ch] is still in use today. Other nearby sights include the baroq[ue] church of SS Pietro e Paolo, with its magnificent org[an] (1744), and the church of Santissima Trinita (at the u[p]per end of the former Palazzo Gardesana) which co[n]tains several colourful frescoes dating from around 140[0].

San Zeno di Montagna

From the suburb of Albisano there is a highly wor[th]while excursion which leads up to one of the most bea[u]tiful views of Lake Garda. The poet Gabriele d'Annunz[io] referred to this place as the *Balcone del Garda*. Just 4k[m] (2 miles) further on is the health resort of **San Zeno [di] Montagna**, with several cheap hotels – a good tip f[or] everyone eager to flee the bustle of the shoreline. It's al[so] the perfect base for hiking trips up Monte Baldo.

Several rock drawings dating from the Bronze Age we[re] discovered in 1964 on ★★ **Monte Luppia** (418m/1,370[ft] and over 250 rocks with more than 3,000 drawings ha[ve] since been found. The rocks depicting swords and arm[ed] men are known as *Pietre delle Griselle*, and the ones wi[th] horsemen *Pietre dei Cavalieri*. The Monte Luppia Ro[ck] Drawings can be reached via the road to Albisano.

Just north of the Bay of Garda, the small promontory th[at] is actually an extension of the Monte Baldo is one of [the] most delightful parts of Lake Garda: the ★★ **Punta Sa[n] Vigilio**. The 16th-century Renaissance patrician Agosti[no]

Punta San Vigilio delights

Brenzone had an elegant villa built here in the middle of a magnificent park; unfortunately it is still privately owned today and closed to public access. The house can still be viewed from the avenue of cypresses in the park, however; it's a Renaissance dream come true. The chapel of San Vigilio can only be visited on 25 April each year.

Pizza express

Continue southwards to the little town of ★ **Garda** (pop. 600), much appreciated for its medieval streets, trendy boutiques and elegant lake promenade. The exorbitantly high prices in the restaurants and clothes shops don't seem to put people off at all – it must be said straight away that Garda is not the cheapest place in the world. The Rocca di Garda, a 294-m (964-ft) high rocky plateau, stands above the town like some oversized tower. Theodoric, king of the Ostrogoths, had a fortress built on top of it in the 5th century, but a few foundation walls are all that remains of it today. The tower played an important role in Italian history: it was here that Adelheid, the widow of King Lothar, was held captive by his successor, Berengar II, before she was rescued by King Otto the Great in 951. Otto duly took Adelheid for his second wife, and they were crowned emperor and empress 11 years later, in 962.

61

Garda is full of noble villas and palazzi, most of which are privately owned. The finest one in town is the **Palazzo dei Capitani** with its Gothic pointed-arch windows, in the Piazza Catullo on the lake promenade. The parish church of **Santa Maria Maggiore** in the Piazzale Roma outside the old town has a fine 15th-century cloister.

A good excursion destination from Garda is **Eremo Monastery**, founded in the 17th century; it's such a strict place that women still aren't allowed anywhere near it. To get there turn off at an Agip petrol station just outside Bardolino and travel as far as the village of Cortelline. There's a tiny road on the left near a statue of the Virgin which leads straight there.

The 16th-century pilgrimage church of ★ **Madonna della Corona**, is perched precariously 774m (2,538ft) above the Adige Valley. To get there, go via Costermano, which has one of the largest World War II military cemeteries in Italy with over 22,000 graves. The church can be reached easily via Caprino Veronese, Spiazzi and then a short walk of around 1km (½ mile), unless you prefer the shuttle bus. The first chapel was built here in 1530, and heaving the construction materials up the mountainside must have been a very arduous business; in 1988 Pope John Paul II was driven right up to the church door in his luxury limousine. Serious pilgrims take the amazingly steep route via the 450 steps which lead from the Adige Valley up to the church.

Bardolino

Lazing around in Lazise

Romanesque San Severo

Guarding the town gate

Next on this route is ★ **Bardolino** (pop. 6,200), at th centre of a wine region famed for its delicious Italia reds that are easily on a par with *Chianti* or *Barolo*, a can be judged at one or more of the numerous tasting along the *Strada del Vino* which makes its well-signposte way past 54 different vineyards. Highlights of the town Bardolino include the Romanesque church of ★ **Sa Severo**, with its mighty campanile. The renditions courtly battles, the Passion and the Apocalypse are ama ingly lifelike. Beyond the high altar the crypt has been e cavated to reveal an earlier Lombard structure. The chap of **San Zeno** (Via San Zeno 13–15) is tucked away in courtyard, but don't miss it: the building dates from th 9th century, and is one of the oldest surviving Carolingia structures in Italy.

The romantic little town of ★ **Lazise** (pop. 5,500) has son well-preserved walls and a six-towered Scaligeri cast (12th-century, privately owned); under Venetian rule was the most important trading post on the lake and al the first independent commune. A 14th-century Vene ian custom house and the 12th-century Romanesqu church of **San Niccolò** both still stand as reminders Lazise's heyday. For something a bit different, why n take the children to see the full-size replica dinosaurs the **Garda Safari Park** at Pastrengo?

The former fishing village of **Peschiera del Garda** (po 8,800) has also been strategically important since R man times, and the 2.3-km (1½-mile) long bastion wal around its old centre were first built during Venetian time and later strengthened by Napoleon and the Austrians. T best way to appreciate their sheer size is to take a bo trip along the moats.

The town of ★★★ **Sirmione** (pop. 5,600) is like something straight out of a fairytale. It lies at the very end of a flat, 4-km (2½-mile) long peninsula which widens at the end to form three rocky crags rising from the brilliant blue of the water. The bright colours of the flowers, and the green of olives, laurels and cypresses combine with the red of the rooftops and the soft light to create a unique Mediterranean atmosphere, all of it set against the incomparable beauty of the high Alps in the distance.

The old centre can either be reached along the peninsula road, with its hotels and supermarkets, or more romantically by boat from Desenzano. The first sight that strikes visitors here is the forbidding-looking ★★ **Scaligeri moated castle**, without a doubt the best-preserved fortress in all Italy. It was built by Mastino I della Scala in 1250, above the foundations of the former Roman harbour. A massive 30-m (98-ft) high keep towers above the castle walls, and there's a stunning ★ panorama from the top that takes in the peninsula and the whole southern half of Lake Garda. The **castle museum** (April to September daily 9am–12.30pm and 2–6pm, October to March Tuesday to Sunday 9am–1pm) contains several finds from antiquity and also a 15th-century Venetian galley.

Sirmione's Scaligeri castle

The old town, with its jumble of alleyways and picturesque houses, is reached through just one gate, and the lake can be glimpsed now and then between the buildings. The whole place gets less busy at the thermal baths – an ugly, purpose-built structure – and there are several gardens on the way down to the Grotte di Catullo. High up on the nearby hill is the small Romanesque church of ★ **San Pietro in Mavino**, built by Lombard monks in the 8th century; the frescoes date from the 12th to the 16th centuries, and there is a particularly impressive *Last Judgement* (daily 9am–sunset).

San Pietro in Mavino

At the very end of the peninsula are the remains of an enormous Roman villa (230m/750ft long, 105m/345ft wide), the so-called ★★ **Grotte di Catullo**. Little appreciated in his day because of his somewhat daring amorous verse, Catullus (87–54BC) knew of this complex of buildings, which was probably an imperial guest house or even an imperial palace, complete with its own thermal baths. He was far too poor ever to have lived here, however. A large swimming pool in the vast complex was fed by the Boiola springs on the lake shore via lead piping. The sulphurous springs were rediscovered in the 16th century, but only re-used 300 years later. Since that time, visitors to Sirmione have been able to enjoy the Ancient Roman pleasure of bathing in hot spring water. The small museum (summer daily except Monday 9am–6pm, winter 9am–4pm) provides a good idea of what the Roman complex must have looked like.

Grotte di Catullo

8b: Southern end of the lake – Battle sites

Peschiera del Garda – Custoza – Solferino – San Martino della Battaglia – Sirmione (60km/40miles)

These days there are no sounds of battle to spoil the tranquillity of the plain south of Sirmione, which is one of the best-kept secrets of Lake Garda. There are reminders of the wars of liberation against the Austrians all over the place, in villages such as Custoza and Solferino. The latter battle, fought in 1859, was so bloody that it resulted in the formation of the Red Cross. This round trip can also be done in bad weather, and if so it should be combined with a trip across to Verona to view the sights there.

Before following the River Mincio across its green meadows, take a short detour to the tiny **Laghetto di Frassino** and to one of the most delightful pilgrimage churches in the region, ★ **Madonna del Frassino**, built in the early 16th century. Legend has it that the Virgin Mary appeared in an ash tree *(frassino)* here in May 1510 and saved a wine farmer from a poisonous snake. The side-chapel containing a miracle-working Madonna sculpture is filled with thousands of candles. From the church, the route continues southeastwards at the little village of Salionze.

Surrounded by meadows and vineyards, ★ **Custoza** lies on a small rise. Former battle sites such as these are known in Italy as *Zona Sacra*, or 'holy zones'. The monument with its enormous obelisk, commemorating the death of thousands of soldiers, can be seen from afar. It was in July 1848 that Count Radetzky's Austrian troops inflicted a crushing defeat on Italy's freedom-fighters. An *ossarium* (daily except Tuesday, November to February 9am–noon and 2–4pm, March and October 9am–noon and 2.30–5pm, April to September 9am–noon and 3.15–7pm) to house the remains of the fallen was built here 30 years later; it contains the bones of 3,200 soldiers of both nations.

The next stop on this route is ★★ **Borghetto di Valeggio sul Mincio**, a sleepy village in the shade of Valeggio's Scaligeri castle which was chosen 600 years ago

Custoza and its ossarium

64

ROUTE 8b
0   5km

s the site of a demonstration of power. In 1393 Gian-aleazzo Visconti decided to build a gigantic dam to de-rive the cities of Mantua and Verona of water. The dimensions are amazing: the ★★ **Ponte Visconteo**, as the dam is called, is 600m (2,000ft) long, 26m (85ft) wide and 10m (32ft) high, and it took just eight months to build. It's worth taking a stroll across the dam, with its gates and tow-ers, to get a close-up impression of this astonishing me-ieval achievement.

In 1438 not even the Venetians dared attack the Ponte Visconteo to help besieged Brescia fight the Visconti. In-tead, Venice was clever and bold enough to transport its warships across the mountains – and then re-float them near Torbole. Imagine the scene: 2,000 oxen pulling 6 gal-leys, 2 galleons and 26 barques across the Nago Pass to Lake Garda! Those interested in learning more about this amazing feat should visit the exhibition at the castle in Malcesine (*see page 58*).

One good nearby excursion destination is the ★★ **Parco Giardino Sigurtà** (Thursday, Saturday, Sunday and pub-lic holidays March to November 9am–6pm), an English-style park in Veneto covering 50 hectares (123 acres). Small lakes, viewing terraces, a hermitage church and yet another ruined Scaligeri castle – they're all here. Every-thing about the place is sheer paradise in fact, except the admission fee.

Solferino

It was at the bloody battle of ★ **Solferino** in June 1859 (*see page 11*) that Henri Dunant, a merchant from Geneva, decided to found the Red Cross (*Croce Rossa*). He received the Nobel Peace Prize for his efforts in 1901, and promptly donated the prize money to his organisation. The great hu-manist did not live to see the horrors of World War I; he died in 1910 in Appenzell. The **Chiesa San Pietro in Vin-coli** contains the remains of around 7,000 soldiers who fell here. By way of contrast, the **Museo Storico** (daily except Monday, March to October 9am–12.30pm and 2.30–8.30pm, winter 9am–noon and 2.30–5pm) documents the glorious side of war, with plenty of weapons, uniforms, etc. The ★ **Piazza Castello**, one of the finest squares in the province of Mantua, was formerly occupied by an 11th-century castle. All that remains of the original building to-day is one watchtower with an oriental-style pointed cupola. The marble Red Cross Memorial, erected here in 1959, can be reached along an avenue of cypresses.

The last famous battle site in this region is **San Mar-tino della Battaglia**, which shared Solferino's fate in 1859. A 74-m (242-ft) high tower stands in memory of the hor-rors of war. Inside, wall frescoes document the history of the Italian freedom fighters from 1848 to 1870.

Remnants of battle at
San Martino della Battaglia

8c – The Western Shore

Desenzano del Garda – Salò – Gardone Riviera · Limone – Riva (70km/44 miles) *See map, p56*

From Salò to Riva alone, a total of 70 tunnels had to b blown out of the rock to build the road along Lake Garda' western shore. Car drivers may be rather confused at a the light and shade, but passengers will glimpse a whol series of superb Mediterranean-style vistas. Even in heav traffic the route can easily be covered in an hour, not in cluding detours. Visiting only a few of the sights can eas ily take up a day, however.

Desenzano del Garda harbour

Restoring Roman mosaics

Desenzano drifters

The town of ★ **Desenzano del Garda** (pop. 23,000) at th southwestern end of Lake Garda is the largest and also th liveliest community on the lake. A harbour since Roma times, the town is still a busy trading centre. Its enormou market is held every Tuesday on the Cesare Battisti lak promenade; the selection of wares is vast, and the price are very reasonable. A few steps away from the mai square, at the end of the Via Crocefisso, are the ruins o a ★ **Villa Romana** dating from the 3rd century AD (Marc to mid-October Monday to Saturday 8.30am–7pm, Sun day and public holidays 9am–6pm; mid-October to Fet ruary Monday to Saturday 8.30am–4.30pm, Sunday ar public holidays 9am–4pm). The 240sq m (2,600sq ft) o mosaic floor reveal the sheer magnificence of Roma lifestyles during Late Antiquity. It's also worth visiting th 16th-century cathedral of **Santa Maria Maddalena** c the Piazza del Duomo; it contains an impressive early wo by Tiepolo, *The Last Supper*, in a side chapel, as well a murals by the Venetian artist Andrea Celesti.

Lonato (pop. 11,400) is a typical Lombard town 10k (6 miles) to the west of Desenzano. It was here in 179 that Napoleon inflicted a crushing defeat on the Austrian

here is a fine view across the Plain of Lombardy from e ruined fortress. On the way up there you'll pass the **Casa del Podestà** (Saturday, Sunday and public holidays 10am–noon and 2.30–7pm, winter till sunset; Monday to Friday by prior arrangement only, tel: 030 913 060), which was richly furnished during the 19th century with furniture, paintings and over 30,000 books by the politician, historian and art collector Ugo da Como.

Just 5km (3 miles) north of Lonato is the wonderfully peaceful ★ **Abbazia di Maguzzano**, a formerly Benedictine abbey built in the 9th century, destroyed in 922 by the Huns and then plundered yet again by the Visconti in the 14th century. It received its present appearance in the 5th century, and the church and cloister are quite magficent. Dissolved by Napoleon in 1797, the abbey fell to decay before being rescued in 1904, when it was purchased by the Cistercian Order.

North of Desenzano is the rolling landscape known as the Valtenesi, a fertile region famous for its pale red *chiaretto* wines. Ruined fortresses on the hilltops testify its violent past, however. **Moniga del Garda**, hidden behind its battlemented walls, is one of the most attractive Valtenesi communities. **Manerba del Garda** is a tourist centre, and there's a good view to be had from the ruined **Rocca di Manerba** (218m/715ft) near Montinelle. Don't miss the 15th-century pilgrimage church of ★ **Santa Maria del Carmine**, situated 13km (7 miles) north of Pieve Vecchia in the middle of a vineyard region; it contains a fine *Annunciation* by a local 15th-century artist as well as a delightful wooden Madonna.

Manerba from the Rocca

Continue now to the delightful town of ★★ **Salò** (pop. 9900). Most of its architectural treasures survived the earthquake of 1901 unscathed, and a stroll here is very worthwhile. Start off at the 15th-century cathedral of **Santa Maria Annunziata** (daily 8am–noon and 1–6pm), the most important Late Gothic structure in the region. Note the 11-m (36-ft) high Gothic-Venetian dome, which measures 44m (144ft) across. Highlights inside include a late Gothic crucifix dating from 1449, and an interesting *St Antony of Padua* by Romanino (1486–1562), in which the artist breaks with convention by portraying his patron most unflatteringly as a fat, unpleasant-looking man at St Antony's feet. Also by Romanino is a *Madonna and Child with Saints Bonaventura and Sebastian*.

Salo: Santa Maria Annunziata

Through a magnificent arcade built by the Venetian architect Sansovino, are the 14th-century Palazzo del Podestà (town hall) and the 16th-century Palazzo della Magnifica Patria, which today houses the **Museo Civico Archeologico** (Monday to Friday 9am–12.30pm and 3–6pm, Saturday 9am–12.30pm, July to September Saturday afternoon and Sunday morning also).

Salò is also famous – or rather infamous – historicall
as the place where Mussolini's Nazi-supported puppe
government continued to rule a reluctant Italy from 194
onwards; its sphere of influence dwindled steadily as th
German troops were forced back. When the German fro
in northern Italy finally crumbled, Mussolini was force
to flee to Switzerland with his mistress Clara Petacci. The
were caught by partisans in Dongo, on Lake Como, an
summarily executed in Mezzegra (*see page 41*).

The town of ★ **Gardone Riviera** (pop. 2,400) no longe
resembles the fishing village it once was, mainly becaus
of the German architect Ludwig Wimmer who built th
Grand Hotel Gardone Riviera here in 1880. The upper pa
of town contains the **Vittoriale** (April to Septembe
8.30am–8pm, October to March 9am–12.30pm and 2
5.30pm, Saturday and Sunday to 6pm), a bombastic mor
ument commissioned just before the war by Fascist Italy
most celebrated poet, Gabriele d'Annunzio. The room
are an amazing mixture of priceless antiques and glorifie
kitsch; in short, the Vittoriale is a gloomy monument to i
owner's megalomania. The complex includes a theatr
a columned hall with the owner's tomb, a domed structur
for the private plane d'Annunzio used to distribute leafle
above Vienna in 1918, a museum full of memorabilia, an
also a ship – or rather the bow section of one. It is pa
of the battleship *Puglia*, filled with cement and uncar
nily realistic.

By way of a change, only a few steps away from th
Vittoriale is the wonderfully peaceful ★ **Giardino Botar
ico** (15 March to 15 October 9am–noon and 2–6pm).
was laid out in 1910, and its waterfalls, ponds and bridge
make it an oasis of tranquillity.

Botanical delights at Gardone

Sant'Andrea

The main attraction of **Toscolano-Maderno** is the 12th
century parish church of ★★ **Sant'Andrea**, on the lak
promenade in Maderno. Fragments of an Early Christ
ian temple and also the remains of an earlier Lombar
structure can be recognised from the facade, apse and wes
work. The entrance portal has some very fine sculptur
work. Toscolano, the other half of this twin-town, gre
rich during medieval times by making metal componen
for Venetian galleys, and then even richer from its pape
and printing industry which started here in the 15th cer
tury and is still flourishing today.

The picturesque town of ★ **Gargnano** (pop. 3,300) has s
far been left relatively unscathed by tourism. From 194
to 1945 the neoclassical Palazzo Feltrinelli housed th
ministries of the fascist 'Republic of Salò'; today it i
where Milan University holds its language courses durin

Villa Feltrinelli

e summer. Fifty years ago Mussolini lived in the **Villa Feltrinelli**, just a short walk away; today it's closed to public access. Another highlight of Gargnano is the so-called 'stone lemon garden' (late July to late August daily 0am–1pm and 3–8pm, otherwise 9am–6pm) in the late 13th-century Romanesque-Gothic cloister of San Francesco, where citrus fruit can be seen adorning the capitals in place of the usual demons and gargoyles.

For adventurous motorists, there's a nice excursion from Gargnano to the 13th-century (later baroquefied) pilrimage church of ★★ **Madonna di Monte Castello**. Situated 700m (2,290ft) above sea level, it lies at the end of a road full of bends, and there's a brief gradient of 26 percent just before you arrive. The church was built above the ruins of a Scaligeri fortress, and the ★★ view is absolutely incredible. From here, continue on to ★ **Tremosine**, the collective name for several villages in the wild and romantic Campione valley. Many coins and also the 'Stone of Voltino', with Latin and Etruscan inscriptions now in the Roman Museum in Brescia, were found here, testifying to settlement of this region as far back as antiquity. In those days it was used as a place of refuge, and today the area is still off the beaten track; its hairpin bends continue to deter tourist buses.

Madonna di Monte Castello

69

A warning at this point to all motorists without a head for heights: the roads often pass amazingly steep drops and require not only good nerves but also good driving abilities. In bad weather they should be avoided completely because of the danger of falling rocks. Just remember that the Italian word for 'gorge' is *orrido*...

Of all the small villages with incredibly good views around here, **Pieve** deserves special mention. Those prone to vertigo should avoid dining in Pieve's 'Miralago' restaurant, despite the excellent food the restaurant terrace juts out above a vertical drop of 350m (1,148ft).

You need a good head for heights

Hooting before each hairpin on the way back from Pieve to the road round the lake isn't just recommended – it's obligatory. The narrow road, lined with waterfalls and vines, is just wide enough for one car.

Back down at the lake, the town of **Limone sul Garda** is not what it once was. Formerly the lemon garden of Lake Garda, it has now sold its soul completely to tourism, and the *limonaie* (greenhouses for lemon-growing) that once cheered the place up are very thin on the ground these days. The old parish church of **San Benedetto** (17th-century) in the centre is worth a visit for Andrea Celesti's *Three Magi* on the right of the altar. By the way, don't leave Limone sul Garda without sampling its delicious carp dishes, flavoured – of course – with lemon.

Limone sul Garda

8d – Some Smaller Lakes

Gargnano – Lago di Valvestino – Lago d'Idro – Lago di Ledro (80km/50 miles) *See map, p56*

If the noisy shores of Lake Garda prove too much of a strain on the nerves, what better way to wind down than to take a trip to some of Lombardy's smaller lakes? Generally speaking, mass tourism has passed them by. This route leads from Gargnano on Lake Garda to the Lago di Valvestino (actually a reservoir) near Gargnano, on to the Lago d'Idro which only has communities along its western bank, up to the tiny Lago di Ledro with its prehistoric pile dwellings and then back to Lake Garda. Allow three hours for the trip.

Fishing on Idro

Flowers for sale

From Gargnano, travel the short distance to **Lake Valvestino**, a reservoir set between the Val Toscolano and the valley of the Valvestino. The shimmering green, fjord-like waters of the lake contrast most impressively with the dam, and the whole scene is framed against magnificent mountain scenery. There are great views to be had from the top of Monte Caplone, reached from Magasa.

The next lake on the route is the ★ **Lago d'Idro**, known to the Romans as the *Lacus Eridius*. The steep mountain cliffs that surround the Lago d'Idro seem to rise straight out of the water in places, and some sections of shore are impassable. Situated 368m (1,207ft) above sea level, the lake is roughly 10km (6 miles) long, up to 2km (1 mile) wide, and 122m (400ft) deep. The Lago d'Idro is the highest of all the Italian lakes, but its water temperature is astonishingly similar to that of Lake Garda, reaching around 25°C (77°F) during the summer. It is particularly renowned for its trout.

Lake Idro is particularly popular with campers, and there are several sites dotted around the main resort village of **Idro**; one of the best is the Campeggio Venus. The nearby village of **Anfo** is rather more attractive than Idro itself, and is very popular with sailing enthusiasts. Just outside the village, up on the **Rocca d'Anfo**, is a castle originally built by the Venetians during the 15th century; since then it has undergone quite a lot of alteration. In 1866 Garibaldi used it as his headquarters, and during World War I it was used for military purposes again in the fight against the Austrians. The small chapel of **Sant'Antonio** nearby contains 15th- and 16th-century frescoes, but is usually closed. Ponte Caffaro, 2km (1 mile) before the northern tip of the lake, is where the Counts of Lodrone did battle first with the Milanese and then the Venetians, and Italy's former border with the then Austrian-ruled Trentino used to be located here until 1918.

There's a good detour 16km (10 miles) westwards at this point to ★★ **Bagolino**, which was very wealthy in medieval times because of the iron ore mined in this valley. The detour there begins with several superb views across the lake, and Bagolino not only has some fine churches but also several magnificent town houses, reflecting the prosperity of its medieval population.

Continue along the western shore of Lake Idro now and at Ca Rossa, turn right on to the road leading to Lake Ledro. This route takes you through the Val d'Ampola, past several waterfalls and high mountain peaks (Monte Cadria, 2,254m/7,395ft) as it winds its way steadily uphill. From Tiarno the road then descends again to ★ **Lake Ledro**.

Coffee time

Lake Ledro is only 3km (2 miles) long, 1km (½ mile) wide and up to 48m (150ft) deep, but is surrounded by some stunning mountain scenery and is also important historically as the site of several lake dwellings. For centuries the fishermen of Lake Ledro were irritated by the wooden stakes that kept getting caught in their nets, but no-one realised what the wood was actually doing there. When the water level was lowered in 1929 during a hydroelectric project the remains of over 15,000 piles were discovered. It turned out that people had lived here in 1700BC in a prehistoric village on the lake, and the piles had supported the entire structure. Pottery and other finds are on display in the ★ **Lake Dwelling Museum** (March to June and September to November daily except Monday 9am–noon and 2.30–6pm; July to August 9am–noon and 3–7pm; December weekends only 9am–noon and 2–5pm; January and February closed) in the village of **Molina di Ledro**.

From Lake Ledro it's not far to the Cascata del Ponale waterfall and back to Lake Garda.

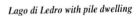

Lago di Ledro with pile dwelling

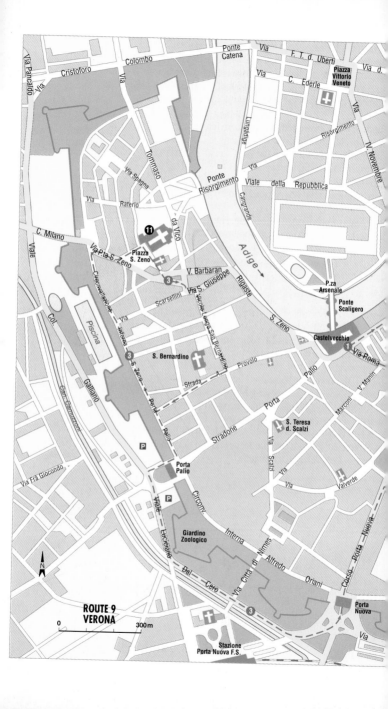

Via Pancaldo
Cristoforo
Colombo
Ponte Catena
Via
F. T. d. Uberti
Via d.
C. Ederle
Piazza Vittorio Veneto
Via
Via
Tommaso
Via Spagna
Via
Raterio
Lungadige
Cangrande
Risorgimento
IV Novembre
Ponte Risorgimento
Viale della Repubblica
C. Milano
Viale
Col.
da Vico
11
Piazza S. Zeno
Via P.ta S. Zeno
3
V. Barbaran
Via S. Giuseppe
Rigaste
Adige →
Scarsellini
Chiesa di Baldaria
Via Riforma
Lungo San Bernardino
P.za Arsenale
Ponte Scaligero
Castelvecchio
1 Via Roma
Piscina
3
S. Bernardino
Provolo
S. Zeno
Via Cattaneo
Galliano
Strada
A
Porta
Palio
Marconi
V. Manin
Via Frà Giocondo
Pallò
Stradone
S. Teresa d. Scalzi
Via Scalzi
Via
Valverde
P
Porta Palio
P
Viale Luciano
Circonv.
Interna
Giardino Zoologico
Dal Cero
Via Città di Nimes
Alfredo
Oriani
Corso Porta Nuova
Porta Nuova
3
Via
ROUTE 9 VERONA
0   300m
Stazione Porta Nuova F.S.
N

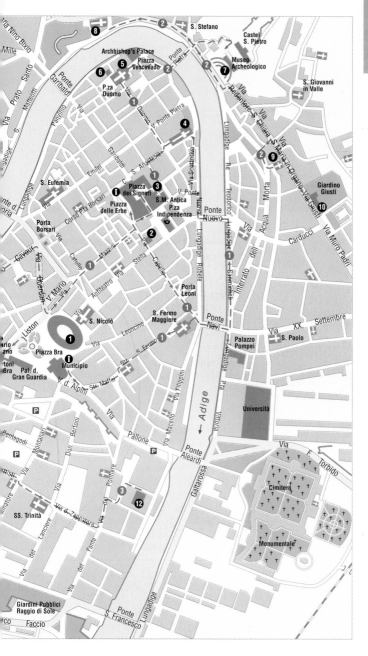

Wet night at the Opera

Route 9

Verona

Juliet's house

Situated on a sharp bend in the River Adige, Verona
an ancient city with Roman remains that are second on
to those of Rome itself. It was also a renowned centre
painting in medieval times, but is perhaps most famous
all as the backdrop to Shakespeare's *Romeo and Juliet*

History

Verona is located at a point of great strategic significance
at the junction of main roads between Italy and Europe.
89 BC it became a Roman colony, and this marked the sta
of its 'Golden Age', which lasted as long as Roman ru
itself: from the 1st century BC to the 5th century AD. Du
ing this time *Colonia Augusta* received its municipal cha
ter, became the capital of Cisalpine Gaul and develope
into an important trade and administration centre. Aff
the Romans left it was occupied by the Visigoths, then t
Byzantines, and then the Lombards. After a Carolingia
interlude the Lombards returned once more.

Medieval times were beset by feuds between rival fam
ilies. In 1277 the della Scalas gained the upper hand an
ruled for over a century. It was during this period that t
Scaligeri castles were built which have been such a stri
ing feature of the region to this day. Peace returned wh
Verona voluntarily submitted to Venetian domination
1405, and it continued until the arrival of the French
1796. After Napoleon's defeat in 1814, Verona found
self in Austrian hands and the fortifications were strengt
ened. 1866 brought Italian unification, and although t
Austrians still clung on until 1914, their final hopes we
dashed by the outbreak of World War I.

This tour begins at the **Piazza Brà**. It's the longest of the three and also contains the most sights, so half a day would be best. Entrance fees are usually charged for the sights. *Chiese Vive*, an association of several churches, offers a combined ticket, which is cheaper.

Piazza Brà facade

Verona's famous ★★ **Arena ❶** (daily except Monday 9am–7pm; during summer festival July and August 9am–2pm only), built in 50BC, is the second largest in the world after the Coliseum in Rome. Originally it was 152m (715ft) long, 123m (403ft) wide and could accommodate 30,000 spectators. Today, two thousand years and several earthquakes later, it is still 138m (452ft) long and 109m (357ft) wide, and still has room for 20,000 people.

Arena arches

Even those with very little time to sightsee should definitely not miss ★ **Castelvecchio**, the largest structure dating from Scaligeri times, which today houses the ★ **Museo di Castelvecchio** (daily except Monday 9am–6.15pm), Verona's most famous art museum. It contains works by masters of the Veronese and Venetian schools from the 13th to the 18th century (paintings by Pisanello, Veronese, Mantegna and Tintoretto), all hung magnificently.

Museum exhibit

75

At the end of the Via Mazzini, Verona's most elegant shopping street, is the ★ **Casa di Giulietta ❷** (daily except Monday 9am–6.30pm, longer in summer) with the most famous balcony in the world (Via Capello No 23), where Shakespeare's Juliet is supposed to have lived.

Today's picturesque ★★ **Piazza delle Erbe** used to be the old Roman forum, and the architecture here is wonderfully harmonious. The Gothic Colonna del Mercato is a 14th-century obelisk built under the Visconti rule; the Capitello, a late 15th-century marble baldachin in the centre of the square, was used as an official meeting-place and also as a pillory in its time. The market fountains also merit attention, as do the various official and very elegant palazzi all round the square.

A high arch, the Arco della Costa, marks the entrance to the ★ **Piazza dei Signori**. The Venetian governor used to reside in the Renaissance Palazzo del Tribunale (1530). Today the Palazzo del Governo is the seat of the provincial government. Dante lived here in 1303, and the café named after him, next door to the magnificent Loggia del Consiglio, is a good place to soak up the impressive atmosphere. The next small square, the Piazzaletto delle Arche, contains the Gothic graves of the Scaligeri, the ★ **Arche degli Scaligeri ❸**, concealed behind wrought-iron grilles. There are even some set into the facade of the 12th-century Romanesque church of Santa Maria Antica. By the way, **Romeo's house** (12th-century) is just a stone's throw away, at Nos 2–4, Via Arche Scaligeri.

Arche degli Scaligeri

*Basilica Sant'
Anastasia, detail*

The ★ **Basilica Sant'Anastasia ❹** was completed i
the 15th century at the end of the arcaded Via Sottoriva b
the Dominican Order. It contains Pisanello's celebrated *S
George Fresco* (15th-century) to the right of the mai
choir. Not far away is the ★ **Cathedral of Santa Mari
Matricolare ❺**, originally a Romanesque structure bui
above a 5th-century Early Christian church. Don't mis
the superbly colourful ★ *Assumption of the Virgin* by Ti
ian in the first side-chapel to the left.

Next door to the cathedral is the ★★ **Biblioteca Ca
pitulare ❻** (daily except Thursday and Sunday 9.30am–
12.30pm, Tuesday and Wednesday also 4–6pm, close
in July), thought to be the oldest surviving library in th
world, with manuscripts dating from the 4th and 5th cen
turies and wonderful miniatures.

City Tour 2 – Along the Adige

Ponte Pietra

This tour starts on the other side of the **Ponte Pietra** an
leads to the best viewpoints in the city. Walking the rout
takes at least 3 hours, doing it by car takes around 1 hou
(parking spaces are available).

On the other side of the bridge on the left is Santo Stefanc
founded in the 5th–6th century and one of the oldes
churches in Verona, and almost straight ahead are the ru
ins of the **Teatro Romano ❼**. Built in AD10, the Ro
man theatre was used as a quarry in medieval times, the
forgotten about and only re-excavated in the 19th century
Shakespeare plays are often performed in the ruins her
during the summer.

The **archaeological museum** (daily except Monda
9am–7pm) up in the monastery of San Girolamo is wort
visiting not only for the finds but also for the magnifi
cent view across the city.

The 15th-century church of ★★ **San Giorgio Maggior
❽**, with its cupola by Sanmicheli, has been describe
as the finest Renaissance building in Verona. Highlight
inside include a *Baptism of Christ* by Tintoretto and a *Mar
tyrdom of St George* altar painting by Veronese. Durin
his Italian Journey, Goethe noted that San Giorgio wa
'a gallery full of good paintings'.

The next two stops on the tour are further up the Adige
firstly the church of ★ **Santa Maria in Organo ❾**, for
merly Benedictine, which gained its earliest written men
tion in 866, and received its Renaissance splendour fror
Sanmicheli at the end of the 15th century; and secondl
the ★ **Palazzo Giusti ❿** (summer daily 9am–8pm, wir
ter 9am–sunset), a beautifully situated 16th-centur
palazzo, high up above the city in terraced grounds, wit
a stunning panoramic view.

Palazzo Giusti

City Tour 3 – Further Sights

San Zeno Maggiore: bronze door

The starting-point for this tour is the Porta Palio, a city gate dating from the 16th century. Drive round the Circonvallazione to the Piazza San Zeno and the basilica of ★★★ **San Zeno Maggiore** ⑪. Only superlatives can be used to describe this, the most magnificent Romanesque church in Northern Italy. After a previous building on the site was destroyed in the 9th century, the new basilica was completed in 1138 and consecrated to Verona's first bishop and patron St Zeno. The marble sculpture of this Black African saint dating from the 14th century is found at the end of the north aisle; it is venerated by all Veronese as a symbol of their town. Of the incredible number of 12th to 14th-century frescoes inside the basilica, the ★ *Madonna and Saints* triptych by Andrea Mantegna (15th-century) deserves special mention; the music-making angels at the Virgin Mary's feet have marvellously touching expressions.

The facade of the basilica is quite magnificent. The ★★ bronze door with its 48 reliefs and the ★★ stone reliefs by Master Nicolò (12th-century) on either side of the portal are utterly fascinating. Inside, the left-hand side-aisle leads off to a very fine ★ cloister.

The last sight on this route is the ★ **Tomba di Giulietta** ⑫. Legend has it that Romeo and Juliet were secretly married in the former Franciscan monastery on the Via del Pontiere. In the middle of an atmospheric courtyard stands an old fountain into which visitors can throw coins; in the crypt an empty stone sarcophagus is labelled the 'Tomb of Juliet', and regularly receives written petitions from lovers from all over the world. The small museum here is worth a visit though: the **Museo degli Alfreschi** (daily except Monday 8am–7.15pm) has an extensive collection of frescoes and also altar paintings and Roman amphorae.

Juliet's empty tomb

Opposite: Roman Verona

arly Architecture

rchitecture in the Northern Italian Lakes region began
ith early lake dwellings such as those discovered in Lake
edro, not far from Lake Garda. It was around the same
me that the rock drawings appeared on Monte Luppia
nd at Capo di Ponte in the Val Camonica north of Lake
seo. Later the Romans came and left several magnifi-
ent monuments behind; Verona has the second-largest
mount of Roman ruins after Rome itself. The ruined villa
: Desenzano, the thermal baths in Sirmione and the Arena
a Verona all bring antiquity back to life.

The most common material in the lakes region was used
» create its most enduring architectural masterpieces:
tone. One good early example of just how gifted the lo-
al masons were after the collapse of the Roman Empire
the 5th-century baptistery in Riva San Vitale, the old-
st sacred building on Swiss soil.

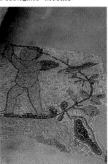

Desenzano mosaic

Romanesque

n the area around Lakes Maggiore and Como during the
2th and 13th centuries, it was the Lombard craftsmen
nown collectively as the *Maestri Comacini* who deter-
ained the local style. These expert stone masons, who
ailed from Como and are known to have been working
t least as long ago as the 7th century, also began to in-
uence styles throughout Europe, establishing a legacy
iat was to continue right up to the Renaissance and
aroque eras. The great baroque architect Francesco Bor-
ominii, who left such a mark on Rome, was himself a
'omo master craftsman.

79

Dark but clearly proportioned churches with richly dec-
rated portals and porches, as well as square bell towers
n the facades are characteristic of the Lombard Ro-
aanesque style. Across in the Garda region, the style
:ached its zenith in buildings like the magnificent basil-
:a of San Zeno Maggiore in Verona (perhaps the finest
.omanesque structure in Northern Italy), San Severo in
ardolino, and San Pietro in Mavino in Sirmione.

San Zeno Maggiore

San Pietro in Mavino

Gothic

riginally created in France, the Gothic style first estab-
shed itself in Lombardy in the middle of the 13th cen-
iry. While the Italian Gothic adopts the French innovation
f the pointed arch, it generally leaves out the exterior fly-
g buttresses, maintaining the solid walls so typical of the
.omanesque. The Lombard builders were not too keen on
ie upwards-striving style of the Gothic, instead prefer-
ng classical horizontal lines and broad interior spaces.
he gradual transition to Gothic is reflected in the cathe-

dral of Santa Maria Matricolare, in Verona. Around lake Maggiore and Garda, the Gothic style seemed to lack the element of courtly chivalry it so thrived upon. However in the cathedral in Salò (1453–1502) and the church of San Francesco in Gargnano (13th-century) are both fine examples of the High Gothic style.

Renaissance

Como cathedral

In around 1400 Florentine builders began to replace the Gothic style by initiating a rebirth of classical motifs and features. Rounded arches, classical columns and great emphasis on the horizontal, achieved for example by cornices, are typical components of the Renaissance style. It gradually made its way across Northern Italy to Lombardy, and Leonardo da Vinci and Bramante were the two artists who helped Renaissance art to flourish here; their students continued the tradition in many buildings and works of art. In the Maggiore region, the most important works dating from the Renaissance period are the facade and choir of Como cathedral, and also Castiglione Olona near Varese, the 'mini-Florence' built in the middle of Lombardy by Cardinal Branda Castiglione.

Veronese statue

In Verona the Renaissance flourished, with architects such as Michele Sanmicheli and Fra Giocondo producing some incomparable work including the portal of Salò cathedral and the Loggia del Consiglio (1485–92) in Verona. Many small rural churches built in the Romanesque and Gothic styles were given Renaissance alterations during this period. The facade of the cathedral of San Lorenzo in Lugano is a good example.

Baroque and neoclassical

Two historical highlights of the baroque era are the parish churches of Limone and Riva on Lake Garda. In Varese the Palazzo Estense is another fine example of the style. The neoclassical movement is best exemplified by the Palazzo Oliginati in Como and the Villa dell'Olmo. During the 19th century Milan assumed a leading role in architectural development; the *Risorgimento* and Italian unification meant that very little was built outside the city. Nevertheless, Varese did receive an attractive art nouveau hotel at the turn of the century, the 'Campo dei Fiori'.

A modern facade

20th-century architecture

During the Mussolini era the pompous style associated with Fascism was accompanied by a very sober and oppressive architecture, best exemplified in Como by the Novocomum (1927–29), the Casa del Fascio (1932–36), the Sant'Elia Kindergarten (1936–7) and the Casa Ascheri (1936). The centre of Locarno was redesigned by Mario Cereghini in 1937.

In the Ticino some modern architecture uses local construction materials, such as granite, very successfully. Mario Botta is one of the more famous exponents of the 'Ticino School'; his Cappella Santa Maria degli Angeli, situated 1,567m (5,140ft) above Lake Lugano, is stunning. Botta's residential houses in the Ticino are designed rather like caves; he refers to them himself as *caverne magiche*. Their strict design is based on mathematical forms such as cubes, prisms and cylinders.

Literature and music

One of the most important Italian poets of the 18th century was the Lombard Giuseppe Parini (1729–99), whose elegant satires were later taken up again by Carlo Porta (1775–1821) in his dialect poetry. Among the 19th-century Romantics, Alessandro Manzoni (1785–1873) from Milan occupies a leading position both because of his historical novels such as *The Betrothed*, set on Lake Como and considered to be the most notable novel in Italian literature, and also because of his religious writings.

Of immense importance for the development of European music as a whole was the introduction of the use of hymns in church by Archbishop Ambrose (339–397) of Milan, who even wrote some hymns himself. In more recent times the development of opera has been closely linked with Lombardy, and with Milan's world-famous Teatro alla Scala in particular. The Bergamo-born Gaetano Donizetti (1797–1848) and Giuseppe Verdi (1813–1901), who chose Milan as his home, Amilcare Ponchielli (1834–86) and Umberto Giordano (1867–1948) are just some of the famous local names to be associated with operatic life in Lombardy. Just as immortal is the name of the star conductor of the Scala, Arturo Toscanini (1867–1957), and of cellist Enrico Mainardi (born 1897).

81

A packed Arena di Verona

Festivals and Folklore

Here are just a few of the many festivals enthusiasticall[y] celebrated throughout the year around the Northern Ital[i]an lakes. Church festivals and processions are not in[-] cluded here, but naturally they provide yet another chanc[e] for a celebration.

Any excuse to celebrate

February	**Carnival in Arco**, with processions an[d] colourful masks to scare away winter, ev[il] spirits, etc.
March	**Festa di mezza quaresime** in Limone, [a] one-day-long break in Lent where me[at] still remains taboo but a great deal of fis[h] and white wine is consumed (especiall[y] deep-fried sardines).
April	The tiny village of San Giulio near Stre[sa] holds its magnificent **flower festiva[l]**; **Good Friday processions** in the villag[es] of Castelletto di Brenzone and Biazza [(a] few miles south of Malcesine), where th[e] Passion is re-enacted by amateur actors [in] torchlit olive groves; the **concert and the[-] atre season** opens in Sirmione and Ma[l-] cesine, with many classical music event[s;] the **Pasqua Musical Arcense** concert fe[s-] tival begins in Arco.
May	**San Filippo Neri** in Torri del Benaco, [a] light festival at the lake in honour of th[e] local patron saint. The festival reach[es] its climax when a boat and thousands [of] floating candles are set alight.
July	**Festa del Pesciolino** in Limone, with fis[h] and white wine served up free in the P[i-] azza Garibaldi during the weeken[d]

Verona: Nabucco performance

celebration. On and around Isola Comacina on the weekend following the feast of St John the Baptist (24 June), the **commemoration of the destruction of the island's city in 1169**, with firework displays symbolising the battle and culminating in a religious procession.

July   **Estiva Jazz**, a jazz festival held in the Piazza della Riforma in Lugano, where jazz greats from all over the world meet up. **Musical Festival** in Lugano, a classical music festival where young students have the chance to meet and study with famous professional artists, and master classes are accompanied by a concert programme. **Drodesera Festival** in the romantic old part of Dro, near Riva del Garda, featuring modern dance and theatre as part of the Trentino Festival. **Estate Musicale** in Salò, a series of classical concerts.

World music in Lugano

Local singer

83

uly/August   **Opera Festival in Verona**, the major cultural event of the year in the Garda region, with bus trips organised to the performances from every major town on Lake Garda, and tickets usually included in the price. Remember, however, that stars such as Pavarotti are totally booked out the moment box offices open.

August   **International Film Festival in Locarno**, held on the Piazza Grande. The best international film is awarded the *Golden Leopard*. **Settimane Musicale** in Stresa, with concert ensembles performing from all over the world. **Festa di Sant'Ercolano**, the festival of the town's patron saint on 11 and 12 August with firework displays in Toscolano-Maderna; on 15 August the **Palio delle Contrade** is held, a big race in traditional lake boats between the various towns around Lake Garda.

September   **Sagra dei Osei**, a whistling and singing contest held on 8 and 9 September in Cisano near Bardolino, in which the competitors have to dress as birds and compete with the real-life birds exhibited.

October   **Festa dell'Uva** wine festivals held on the first weekend of the month in all wine regions around the lakes, e.g. Bardolino. This is the time to buy vast quantities of very good wine cheaply.

ood and Drink

ombard cuisine is as varied as the landscape. The western side of Lake Maggiore belongs to Piedmont, with its uffles, *grissini* and *Barolo*. There are regional specialities here too, of course: a favourite local dish at Lake rta is *tapulon* (minced donkey braised in red wine), and st as delicious is *trotella alla Savoia* (trout on mushrooms).

Local seasoning

Lombardy has some well known traditional favourites, hich also have a great influence on the cuisine in neighbouring Ticino: *ossobuco* (sliced veal braised in white ine), for instance, the unmistakeably yellow *risotto alla ilanese*, or the *costoletta alla milanese*, mentioned in a ombard cookbook dated 1134 as *lombolos cum pani-o*, discovered in the 19th century by the Austrian field-arshal Radetsky and promptly introduced to the Austrian apital as the *Wiener Schnitzel*.

A speciality of the Varesotto is *faraona alla Valcuvia*, artridge Valcuvia-style, formerly baked in a soft clay conainer. Around Verona the *risotto* comes into its own. And or some real Lombard home cooking, why not try a very lling *cazzoeula* (pork stew)?

85

A ubiquitous dish, particularly in the more mountainus areas, is maize pudding or *polenta*. In restaurants it often served with rabbit or as *pancetta con polenta* ured bacon with polenta), but the locals often eat it on s own or with cheese. Maize was only introduced to the gion from America in the 17th century; prior to that le staple of the mountain folk was chestnut porridge.

Fish variation

Fish is of course an integral part of the cuisine around le Italian lakes. *Agonia alla Comasca* (baked and marated shad), *Anguilla del pescatore* (stewed eel), *lavarelli l vino bianco* (white fish in white wine), *pesce in gelatina* ish in aspic) and *suppa di pesce alla tremezzina* (fish up) are just a few of the numerous fish specialities. A ypical Lake Como delicacy is *curadura* (salted and dried nad), a former 'poor man's meal' which has now becomes omething of a gourmet speciality. The delicate Lake arda trout known as *Carpione* should be sampled too.

As far as desserts are concerned one of the best ways wind up a meal Lombard-style is with a *panettone* (yeast ake) from Milan. Another option is to order the wickedly ch *tiramisú*.

Light lunch

Italian cheese is quite delicious, and *gorgonzola* or *bel aese* are always a good bet. Lombard cheese include *rana* (better known to us as Parmesan), *mascarpone* and *racchino*. The *formaggini* (fresh cheeses flavoured with l and hot paprika) from Ticino are particularly good; *ro-iola* comes from the Valsassina and soft *gaprini* comes om the Brianza (which also does very good salami).

Wine comes in a variety of forms

All this talk of cheese naturally leads on to wine. Lombardy is not one of the most important wine regions of Italy, but its reds are particularly good. Top-quality wines come from Piedmont, e.g. *Barolo* (a heavy red). In Ticino the top wine is the ruby-red *Merlot*. Over near Lake Garda, more famous names appear: *Bardolino, Valpolicella* and *Soave* are all grown around Verona, and all delicious. The purple-coloured *Bardolino* comes in varying degrees of quality, and can be tasted all over the place.

One very popular grape in the region south of Lake Garda is the *Trebbiano*, used to make an excellent dry white. A light, fizzy rosé is grown in the Valetnesi region north of Desenzano, and two more fine wines worthy of mention are the heavy white *Tocai del Garda* and the very versatile *Recioto* from the Val Policella. Naturally, a *vino della casa* can always be ordered; they are usually dry, light and 'honest'. One very good one is *Nostrano*, from Ticino.

Here are some restaurants from some of the most popular places mentioned in this guide. They are listed according to three categories: $$$ = expensive, $$ = moderate and $ = inexpensive.

Arona
$$Trattoria Campagna, Via Vergante 12, tel: 0322 57294. Rustic surroundings, very good Italian cuisine.

Downtown Ascona

Ascona
$$Da Ivo, Via Collegio 5, tel: 091 791 1031. Good cooking in an old patrician house.

Bardolino
$$Aurora, Piazzetta S. Severo, tel: 045 721 0038. Veronese cuisine, excellent fish; **$$Il Giardino delle Esperidi**, Via G. Mameli 1, tel: 045 621 0477. Excellent quality food at a reasonable price; **$Al Commercio**, Via Solferino 1, tel: 045 721 1183. Simple and good.

Como cakes and café

Como
$$$Ristorante Raimondi dell'Hotel Villa Flori, Via Cenobbio 10, tel: 031 573105. Elegant restaurant in attractive villa, the noodles with shrimps are very good; **$$Sant'Anna 1907**, Via Turati 1/3, tel: 031 505266. Grilled swordfish is the speciality in this family-run restaurant; **$Tipica Trattoria**, Via Pannilani, tel: 031 261080. Very good seafood.

Desenzano del Garda
$$$Cavallino, Via Murachette 29, tel: 030 912 0217. Top address for gourmets, also does regional dishes.

Garda

$$Locanda di San Vigilio, Punta San Vigilio, tel: 045 25 6688. Elegant restaurant, fine food; **$$Stafolet**, Via Poiano 12, tel: 045 725 5427, closed Tuesday. Good cooking in quiet surroundings; **$Al Pontesel**, Via Monte Baldo 1, tel: 045 725 5419. Pizza and pasta, closed Wednesday.

Gardone Riviera

$$Villa Fiordaliso, Corso Zardelli 132, tel: 0365 20158. This pink villa was Mussolini's mistress's last home, and today is renowned for its seafood dishes.

Gargnano

$$La Tortuga, Via XXIV Maggio 5, tel: 0365 71251. One of the best and also most expensive gourmet restaurants in the region, reservations essential.

Iseo

$Del Doge, Vicolo della Pergola 7, tel: 030 982 1542. Regional specialities and classic dishes, excellent wines; **Il Volto**, Via Matolte 33, tel: 030 981462. A small *osteria* with a lot of tradition.

Laveno

$Lo Scoiattolo, Via Monteggia, tel: 0332 669227. Classic Italian cuisine, summer veranda.

Lazise

$Il Porticciolo, Lungolago Marconi, tel: 045 758 0254, regional cuisine; **$La Forgia**, Lungolago Marconi, tel: 045 647 0372, speciality grilled fish.

Lecco

$$Ristorante al Porticciolo, Via Valsecchi 5/7, tel: 0341 98103. An unforgettable dining experience; **$$$Antica Osteria Enoteca Casa di Lucia**, Via Lucia 27, tel: 0341 94594. Excellent Italian cuisine in an old villa.

Limone sul Garda

$Gemma, Piazza Garibaldi 12, tel: 0365 954014. Good pasta dishes.

Locarno

$$ Centenario, Lungolago Motta 17, tel: 091 743 8222. A mouth-watering gourmet experience. **$$Trattoria da Buigi**, Via Dogana Vecchia, tel: 091 751 9746. Ticino cuisine in pleasant environment; **$$Ca'Nostra**, Brione s/Minusio, tel: 091 743 5852. Excellent Ticino cuisine served on terrace with panoramic view; **$Grott'al Capon**, Brione s/Minusio, tel: 091 331012. Idyllic grotto north of Locarno with good local cuisine.

Cooling off at Garda

Late night in Locarno

Lugano

$$$Saroli, Viale Franscini 8, tel: 091 923 5314. Stylish restaurant with good reputation. **$$$Bianchi**, Via Pessina 3, tel: 091 994 8479. Oldest restaurant in town, with much *grandezza*; **$$La Tinera**, Via dei Giorini 2, tel: 091 92 5219. Delicious Ticino cooking.

Malcesine

$$$Del Park Hotel Querceto, loc Campiano, tel: 045 740 0344. Regional cuisine in elegant surroundings, closed Wednesday; **$$La Toresela**, loc Cassone, Via Chiesa 9, tel: 045 740 0241. Pasta and seafood, closed Monday; **$Pizzeria San Remo**, loc Campagnola, tel: 045 740 0239. Pizza served from clay ovens.

Riva

$$$Vecchia Riva, Via Bastione 3, tel: 0464 555061. Excellent seafood; **$$$Restel de Fer**, Via Restel de Fer, tel: 0464 553481. Lake Garda fish specialities served to folklore performances; **$$Al Volt**, Via Fiume 73, tel: 0464 552570. Nice family-run establishment; **$San Marco**, Via Roma 20, tel: 0464 554477. International cuisine.

Salò

$$Trattoria La Campagnola, Via Brunati 11, tel: 0365 22153. Family-run, home-grown ingredients; **$$Lepanto**, Lungolago Zanardelli 67, tel: 0365 20428. Excellent fish in art nouveau surroundings.

Sirmione

$$$Vecchia Lugana, Lugana, Via Verona 71, tel: 030 919012. One of the top addresses on the lake, regularly praised by food writers; **$$$Rucola**, Vicolo Strentelle 7, tel: 030 916326. Superb cooking; **$$Ancora d'Oro**, loc Colombara, Via d'Aquisto, tel: 030 990 4696. Seafood specialities; **$Osteria del Pescatore**, Via Piana 24, tel: 030 916216. Cheap restaurant in the old part of town.

Dining in Stresa

Stresa

$$$Piemontese, Via Mazzini 25, tel: 0323 30235. The very best Piedmontese cuisine, delicious and expensive; **$$$La Scuderia**, Villa Pallavicino, tel: 0323 31895. Delicious Italian food; **$$L'Emiliano**, Corso Italia 52, tel: 0323 31396. Intimate, elegant restaurant with local cheese specialities; **$$Del Pescatore**, Vicvolo del Poncivo 3, tel: 0323 31986. Good and inexpensive seafood.

Torbole

$$$Piccolo Mondo, Via Matteotti 7, tel: 0464 505271. Great Trentino cuisine, the speciality is a menu consisting entirely of apple dishes; **$$Al Pescatore**, Via Segantini

, tel: 0464 505236. Seafood served in the open air; **$$La rrazza**, Via Benaco 14, tel: 0464 506083. Seafood right eside the lake; **$Aurora**, Via Matteotti 2, tel: 0464 05311. Rustic, inexpensive; **$Cin Cin**, Via Matteotti 3, tel: 0464 505238. Good rice and pizza dishes; **$Ter-azze**, loc Coe, tel: 0464 505301. Trentino specialities and ood wine.

scolano-Maderno

$La Tana, Via Aquilani 14, tel: 0365 644286, closed uesday. Excellent seafood; **$Vecchia Padella**, Via Bianchi tel: 0365 641042. Food served in the garden in summer.

rese

Ristorante Lago Maggiore, Via Carobbio 19, tel: 0331 81183. Finest Italian cooking, especially the seafood.

rbania

$Il Torchio, Via Manzoni 20, tel: 0323 503352. Good alian food, Piedmontese specialities; **$$Osteria dell' ngelo**, Via Garibaldi 35, Palanza, tel: 0323 556362. ood regional specialities in nice surroundings; **$Pizze-a Laguna Blu**, Piazza Matteotti 16, tel: 0323 404289.

rona

$$Arche, Via Arche Scaligere 6, tel: 045 800 7415. losed Sunday and Monday noon, first-class restaurant; **$Il Desco**, Via Dietro San Sebastiano 7, tel: 045 595358. ecommended by all leading Italian food writers; **$$Maf-i**, Piazza Erbe 38, tel: 045 801 0015. Scampi with as-ragus cream is the speciality here; **$$I Dodici Apostoli**, orticella San Marco 3, tel: 045 596999. Try the Venet-n liver, king prawns or rabbit; **$Osteria La Fontan-a**, loc. Santo Stefano, tel: 045 913305. Cheap and cosy.

89

Comings and goings in Verona

High season on Lake Garda

Active Holidays

Angling

Official angling licences have to be procured. They a▮
valid throughout Italy for three months, and cost L60,00▮
The respective local authorities then issue angling permit▮
Fishing without a permit is subject to a high fine. More i▮
formation is available from tourist authorities.

Hiking and climbing

The mountains around Lake Garda are served by wel▮
marked paths and mountain huts (*rifugio*), and include th▮
Monte Baldo high-level route and Monte Pizzocolo abo▮
the western shore. The mountains of Ticino and aroun▮
Lake Como are also easily accessible; around Lake Ma▮
giore the routes are often more difficult to find. Hikin▮
maps can be obtained from the local tourist offices (ATP▮

The centre of mountain climbing in the Garda regio▮
is Arco, a few miles from the northern tip of the lak▮
The mountains around Maggiore provide climbing fa▮
with routes of varying degrees of difficulty. Near Com▮
the paradise for climbers is definitely the Grigna, nor▮
of Lecco; the town itself also has a renowned climbin▮
school that does several courses in mountaineering.

Ready for the road

Cycling

The Italians have always been very keen cyclists, an▮
numerous *Girini* can be seen around the lakes, primaril▮
at weekends. Bicycles *(biciclette)* can be hired in Ticin▮
at any major rail station. There is a signposted cycle rou▮
from Bellinzona to Ascona. The best routes for cycl▮
are the tiny ones between the lakes, or the flat area sou▮
of Lake Garda in particular. Mountain bikes can also ▮
hired in most places, but remember that a lot of mou▮

in roads are closed between November and mid-April.
tip for the less ambitious: the cable car from Malce-
ne on Lake Garda up to Monte Baldo also takes moun-
in bikes, saving an exhausting ascent and providing you
ith a superb trip back down.

olf

olfers will find excellent courses in Ascona (18 holes),
ugano (18), Carimate (18), Lanzo d'Intelvi (9), Mon-
rfano (18), Appiano Gentile (18), Cassina Rizzardi (36),
a'degli Ulivi (18) and Sommacampagna (near Desen-
no, 18).

ang-gliding

or courses in this at Lugano, the school to contact is the
cuola Volo delta Lugano, tel: 092 822487. Near Lake
arda, the cable railways from Malcesine up to Monte
aldo and from Prada to Costabella take gliders up to
800m (5,900ft), allowing the opportunity to take at least
vo flights a day. The local hang-gliding school in the
arda region is Deltaland, loc. Platano di Caprino
eronese, tel: 045 623 0024.

91

iding

he countryside around the Northern Italian lakes is ideal
or riding trips. Near Garda, the best riding routes are in
e hilly country inland from Garda itself, along the slopes
Monte Baldo, or the river meadows along the Mon-
o. In the Maggiore region, there are riding schools in
osone (near Locarno), Quartino (near Magadino),
ngera, Ghirla (Varesotto), Bodio (Lake Varese) and Ma-
eglio and Canzo (both on Lake Como).

ky-diving

or an exhilarating aerial view of Lake Maggiore, why not
ll out of a plane belonging to either the Club Parapen-
o Ticino in Locarno (tel: 091 752 1558) or the Scuola
olo Libero Lugano (tel: 091 972 5821).

Happy landings

Water sports

indsurfing is available on Lakes Maggiore and Como,
t nowhere is more popular than the northern part of Lake
arda, around Torbole. Here the surfers get blown south-
ards by the *Tramuntana* in the mornings and then up
e lake again in the evenings by the *Ora*. In the summer
onths there are sometimes so many windsurfers around
at ordinary swimming becomes almost impossible; there
ain, the water in the southern part is much warmer for
thing anyway. All the lakes have facilities for every con-
ivable kind of other water sport including diving, wa-
r-skiing and sailing; the larger resorts have schools.

Ideal winds off Torbole

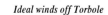

Getting There

By Plane

For Lake Como and Lake Maggiore, the most convenient port of entry is Milan. British Airways and Alitalia each operate 4 flights a day to Milan-Linate Airport from London Heathrow. Direct flights from the US arrive at Milan-Malpensa Airport. Visitors from the UK to the Lake Garda region are advised to fly to Verona; British Airways operates 2 flights a day from London Gatwick. There are no direct flights to Verona from the US, so visitors might consider flying via London. Alternatively, Verona can be reached in a more roundabout manner (a train journey or very expensive taxi ride) from either Venice or Milan.

By train

Train spotters

If travelling direct from the UK, the most convenient place to head for is Milan. Take the Eurostar to Gard du Nord in Paris, then cross to Gare du Lyon for overnight services to Milan through the Simplon Tunnel. Milan is connected by rail to Lake Maggiore, Varese, Como and Bergamo, as well as Brescia, the southern tip of Lake Garda and Verona which are all on the main line to Venice. If arriving from Germany or Austria, another possibility for Lake Garda is via the Brenner Pass, and down to Rovereto or Verona, each of which have direct bus connections to every resort on the lake. For the Maggiore and Como region, there are also hourly trains via Switzerland along the so-called 'Gotthard line'.

93

By Car

Northern Italy is well connected to the rest of Europe by motorway, but it's worth remembering that if you arrive via Switzerland you need to buy a special *vignette* (valid one year, price Sf50).

Drivers must always carry a driving licence, the car registration documents and insurance certificate. Breakdown service is usually free of charge for members of automobile clubs. Seat-belts are compulsory in Italy. Never leave anything in the car which might attract thieves – not even for a few moments. Also, remember that the fines for traffic offences in Italy (parking, speed limits, etc) are high.

The following speed limits apply to motor traffic in Italy unless otherwise indicated: 50kmph (30mph) in built-up areas, 90kmph (55mph) on country roads, and 130kmph (75mph) on motorways (*autostrada*). Speed limits are often lowered at weekends or on public holidays. Police checks have become much stricter in recent times, and excessive speed as well as excessive alcohol consumption can cost motorists their licence – this also applies to foreign drivers.

Getting Around

Skirting Lake Garda

By Car

Without a car it's virtually impossible to see the best th
the lakes have to offer. Renting a car is probably cheap
than bringing your own, and there is no shortage of fl
drive packages, where cars can be collected on arrival. A
ternatively, both international and local car hire firms a
represented in the major centres.

Driving along the narrow, winding mountain roads re
quires care and attention. Remember that the car neare
the mountain has priority. It is customary to use the ho
to warn that you are about to overtake and to warn c
your presence on a blind bend. Many of the roads in th
area, particularly the one along the western shore of Lak
Garda, disappear into tunnels. Here, dipped headlight
must be used.

By Train

Near the lakes themselves, the following connections ar
possible: Locarno–Luino–Laveno–Sesto Calende; Simplon–Stresa–Sesto Calende; Laveno–Varese–Milan
Como–Milan; Como–Lecco; and Milan–Lecco–Colico
As far as tickets are concerned, keep an eye out for the various special offers available from the Swiss (SBB) and
the Italian railways (FS). For connections from Milan to
Lake Garda, remember that the fast express trains don'
stop at Peschiera, Sirmione or Desenzano.

By Bus

There are very good bus networks in Switzerland and Italy,
and reaching destinations usually poses no problems at all.
The local tourist offices can provide timetables and gen-
eral information.

Getting to the other side

By Boat

One of the best and most relaxing ways of seeing the lakes
is from the deck of a steamer. All major towns on the
Italian lakes have ferry connections for passengers, and
a number of towns are linked by car ferry as well: Verbania–Laveno on Lake Maggiore; Menaggio–Bellagio–Varenna and Cadenabbia–Bellagio–Varenna on Lake
Como; and Maderno–Torri del Benaco on Lake Garda).
The Maggiore and Lugano steamers cross the border between Italy and Switzerland, so the usual border proce-
dures apply. The larger vessels have on-board restaurants.
For a trip along the full length of Lake Garda, from Desenzano to Riva, allow around four and a half hours.

Cruises are a regular feature during the summer months,
and disco ships are also common. Genuine old-fashioned
paddle steamers are still used by some operators.

cts for the Visitor

A place for children, too

avel documents

sitors from European Union countries require either a
ssport or identification card to enter Italy. Holders of
ssports from most other countries do not usually require
sas for a period not exceeding three months.

stoms

ere have been practically no customs limits for nationals
EU member states since 1993. The following are just
ugh guidelines: 800 cigarettes, 200 cigars, 1kg of to-
cco, 90 litres of wine.

rrency regulations

limited amounts of foreign currency and Italian lire may
brought in and out of Italy, but need to be declared if
e sum exceeds L20 million.

urist information

ere are the addresses of the Italian Tourist Office (ENIT):
K: 1 Princes Street, London W1, tel: 020 7408 1254.
: 630 Fifth Avenue, Suite 1565, New York NY 10111,
: 212 245 4822.

In Italy, contact the APT (Azienda di Promozione Tur-
ica): APT Verona, Via Leoncino 61, 37121 Verona, tel:
5 806 8680, fax: 045 800 3638; APT Garda/Trentino,
ardini di Porta Orientale 8, 38066 Riva del Garda, tel:
64 554444, fax: 0464 520308; APT Como, Piazza
vour 17, 22100 Como, tel: 031 274064, fax: 031
1152; APT del Varesotto, Viale Ippodromo 9, 21100
rese, tel: 0332 284624, fax: 0332 238093; APT del Lago
aggiore, Via Principe Tomaso 70/72, 28049 Stresa, tel:
23 30150, fax: 0323 32561. APT Bergamo, 20 Viale Vit-
io Emanuele II, tel: 035 213185/242226.

Currency and exchange

The unit of currency in Italy is the lira (abbreviated Lit. or L), which comes in 50, 100, 200 and 500 lire coins and 1,000, 2,000, 5,000, 10,000, 50,000, 100,000 and 500,000 lire notes. Foreign and Italian currency not exceeding 20 million lire in value may be brought in and out of the country; larger sums need to be declared.

Eurocheques can be cashed up to a maximum value of 300,000 lire at banks with the EC symbol. Most credit cards, including Visa, Access and American Express, are accepted in hotels, restaurants and shops and for air and train tickets and cash at any bank. All the larger towns in the region have automatic bank tellers ('Bancomat').

Tipping

This is expected, despite all-inclusive prices (approximately 10 percent).

Bills and receipts

Not only the Italians themselves but also foreign tourists are expected to have receipts (*ricevuta fiscale*) made out by restaurants, hotels, car repair workshops, etc, listing services rendered plus the correct amount of Italian VAT (IVA) and to keep them on their person for possible check by the Italian fiscal authorities. Failure to furnish receipts can often result in a stiff fine.

Opening times

Generally, shops are open on weekdays from 9am–7.30pm with a lunch break from 1–3.30pm. Many shops are closed on Saturday and Monday mornings.

Banks: Monday to Friday 8.30am–1.30pm; some also open in the afternoon from 2.45pm–3.45pm. Money can be exchanged at weekends in the railway stations and airports of the larger cities.

Museum opening hours vary considerably, and the times stated in this book are subject to change. State-owned museums are generally open daily from 9am–2pm, and 9am–1pm on Sunday and public holidays. They are often closed on Monday. Note: some state-owned and municipal museums allow free admission to visitors under and over 60 years of age.

Churches are usually closed around lunchtime, roughly from noon–4pm.

Filling Stations, apart from those on the motorways, are closed at lunchtime and on Sunday and public holidays. Some have cash-operated automatic pumps.

Beachware

Souvenirs

Most souvenirs are of the gastronomic variety, with fine quality olive oil, cheese, truffles, sausages, honey, wine

nd *grappa* usually topping the list. Bargains can also be
ad at flea markets in the larger towns; try to avoid the
numerable boutiques in the tourist resorts. Antiques mar-
ets are also a good place to buy special items cheaply.
sk at the local tourist information outlet about where and
hen they are held.

ublic holidays

January, 6 January (Epiphany), Easter Sunday, Easter
onday, 25 April (National Day of Liberation), 1 May,
hit Sunday, 15 August (Assumption of the Virgin, fer-
gosto), 1 November, 8 December (Immaculate Con-
ption), and 25 and 26 December (Christmas).

In addition, many businesses close at some time during
ugust and whole towns tend to close when a major fes-
val is in progress.

ostal services

ain post offices in major towns are open all day, some
late as 7pm, otherwise the hours are Monday to Sat-
day 8am to 1.30pm. Stamps are sold at post offices as
ell as at bars and tobacconists; look for the white letter
on a blue background.

Post haste

97

elephone

Post-modern phones

alls can be made from phone centres run by the phone
mpany TELECOM (not in post offices) or from coin-
erated public phones either with L100, L200 and L500
ins or with pre-paid phone cards (scheda telefonica)
ailable for L5,000, L10,000 and L15,000 from many
wsagents, tobacconists or from TELECOM offices.

There is direct dialing to most countries. Dialing codes
om Italy: Australia 0061; United Kingdom 0044; US and
anada 001.

If calling within Italy, note that the area or city codes
e now dialled as part of the number even when calling
thin the same city or area. Thus a Como number always
s the code 031 attached no matter where you're call-
g from. And if calling you're calling from abroad, the
' is always retained.

AT&T: 172-1011, Sprint: 172-1877, MCCI: 172-1022.

Hours ahead

me

ly is six hours ahead of US Eastern Standard Time and
e hour ahead of Greenwich Mean Time.

oltage

sually 220v – the voltage is printed on the bulbs. Safety
ugs cannot always be used. Specialist shops can provide
aptors *(spina di adattamento)*; however, owners of
merican appliances will need a transformer.

Nude Sunbathing

Stripping off completely is not allowed. The 'monokin is largely tolerated these days, but there are no nudi beaches on any of the lakes.

Crime

The lakes are relatively free of crime, but visitors shoul still take the usual precautions: don't leave any valuabl inside your car, always lock the vehicle when you leav it, and leave your cash in the hotel safe. When out wal ing in big towns and cities keep a close eye on your car eras and handbags.

The summer crush

Medical

With Form E111 from the Department of Health and S cial Security, UK visitors are entitled to reciprocal me ical treatment in Italy. There are similar arrangemen for other members of EU countries. It may neverthele be advisable to take out insurance for private treatme in case of accident. Holiday insurance policies and priva patients schemes are recommended for non-EU visitor

In case of minor ailments, chemists (*farmacie*) are we stocked with medicines, often sold without prescriptio Farmacie, which are normally open Monday to Frida 9am–1pm and 4–7pm, are identified by a sign displa ing a green cross on a white background. For other time the address of the nearest emergency chemist will k posted in the window.

Emergencies

Emergency Assistance (Ambulance, fire, police), tel: 11
Police Immediate Action, tel: 112.
Breakdown service, tel: 116.
Winding down   Emergency medical assistance, tel: 118.

ccommodation

Vhether you feel like sleeping in a 17th-century villa, a *asa rustico* or out on a campsite, Ticino, Lombardy and iedmont all have a huge variety of accommodation posbilities to suit every taste.

On Lake Maggiore, the luxury hotels tend to be on the wiss side, around Verbania, while smaller, family-run otels are mostly located on the eastern shore. There is xury in abundance, too, on Lake Lugano and around omo, and the hotels are usually magnificent old villas rrounded by extensive parks. Alongside these five-star stablishments there are also numerous medium-priced les that offer cable TV, swimming pools and air condioning. Around Lake Garda there are less of the luxuris five-star hotels that one sees elsewhere.

Generally speaking, the nearer a lake a hotel is, the more kpensive the accommodation. Cheaper logdings can be ound in the towns and villages of the hinterland, away om the lakes, where one can find not only hotels but also :nsions and rooms let out by farmers (*agroturismo*). ampsites are usually right beside the lakes (the ones innd are a lot cheaper and quieter), and generally have l modern conveniences even though they can often be vercrowded in the summer months.

Anyone keen to book a holiday house can organise anying from a *casa rustica* to an enormous villa. More inormation can be obtained from the tourist offices.

otel selection

ere is a selection of hotels from some of the most popar centres. They are listed according to three categories: 5$ = expensive, $$ moderate and $ = inexpensive.

scona

$$**Castello Seeschloss**, Piazza G Motta, tel: 091 791 61. Luxurious hotel situated in old castello; $$**Tamaro**, azza G Motta 35, tel: 091 791 0282. Patrician residence ith attractive inner courtyard and good restaurant.

ardolino

$**Du Lac**, Via S Cristina, tel: 045 621 0355. Has its own each and a fine restaurant; $**Al Parco**, Via Fosse 20, tel: 5 721 0039. Centrally located, not all that quiet.

ellagio

$**Grand Hotel Villa Serbelloni**, tel: 031 950216. omantic luxury hotel in old villa right on Lake Como; $**Fiorini – da Piero**, tel: 031 950392. Good, cheap and mfortable; $**La Pergola**, 031 950263. Simple, clean establishment, family-run.

Villa d'Este in Como

Brissago

$$$Villa Caesar, tel: 091 793 2766. An elegant establishment right beside the lake.

Como

Palace Hotel, Como

$$$Grand Hotel Villa d'Este, Cernobbio, tel: 031 348 A 16th-century villa with five-star luxury; **$$$Palace Hotel**, Lungolario Trieste 16, tel: 031 303303. Four-star establishment by the lake and near the cathedral; **$$$Villa Flori**, Via Cernobbio 12, tel: 031 573105. Top quality hotel with mountain and lake view; **$$Metropole Suisse**, Piazza Cavour 19, tel: 031 269444. Good, reasonably-priced hotel in the centre.

Desenzano del Garda

$$$Lido International, Via Tommaso dal Mulin 43, tel 030 914 1027. A very good hotel; **$$City**, Via Nazari Sauro 29, tel: 030 991 1704. Nice town hotel in a peaceful location; **$Principe**, Via Grigollo 20, tel: 030 912 148. Good for a night.

Garda

Guarding Garda

$$$Du Parc, Via Marconi 3, tel: 045 725 5343. Beautifully situated in a grove of palm trees next to the lake; **$$Flora**, Via Madrina 4, tel: 045 725 5348. Includes sauna, swimming pool and tennis courts, very friendly service; **$Marco Polo**, Via dei Cipressi, tel: 045 725 5335. Cheap and comfortable.

Gardone Riviera

$$$Grand Hotel Gardone Riviera, Via Zanardelli 7 tel: 0365 20261. Luxury establishment with a century of tradition; **$–$$Bellevue**, Via Zanardelli 81, tel: 0365 290088. Very comfortable; **$San Michele**, Via S Michele 26, tel: 0365 20575. A good inexpensive place to stay.

Gargnano

$$$Villa Giulia, Viale Rimebranza, tel: 0365 71022. Quiet location, next to lake; **$Europa**, Via Repubblica 38, tel 0365 71191. Modern establishment, very comfortable.

Laveno

$$Moderno, Viale Garibaldi 15, tel: 0332 668373, fax 0332 666175. Reasonably-priced, medium-category hotel

Limone sul Garda

$$$Park Hotel Imperial, Via Tamas 10, tel: 0365 95459 Five-star luxury, beauty cures, fitness studios; **$$Cristina**, Via Tamas 20, tel: 0365 954641. Nice affordable lodgings; **$Sole**, Lungolago Marconi 26, tel: 0365 954055. Centrally situated, cheap.

ocarno
$$La Palma au Lac, Viale Verbano 29, Locarno Mu-
alto, tel: 091 735 3636. Four-star hotel with piazza and
randezza, right next to the lake; **$$Nessi**, Via Varenna 79,
ocarno-Solduno, tel: 091 751 7741. Hotel built in mod-
rn Ticino style.

Locarno Casino

ugano
$$Grand Hotel Villa Castagnola, Viale Castagnola 31,
•l: 091 971 2213. Beautifully situated by the lake, five-
ar luxury; **$$$Hotel de la Paix**, Via Cattori 18, tel: 091
94 2332. Elegant, grand hotel; **$$Meister**, Via San Sal-
atore 11, tel: 091 993 1720. Pleasant, centrally located
tel.

uino
$$Camin, Via Dante 35, tel: 0332 530118. Elegant ho-
l surrounded by park at the centre of town.

Malcesine
$$Park Hotel Eden, Via Gardesana Navene, tel: 045 657
130. For the very wealthy; **$$Maximilian**, Val di Sogno,
l: 045 740 0317. Quiet hotel in olive grove with tennis
ourt and pool; **$Lago di Garda**, Piazza Matteotti 1, tel:
45 740 0633. Centrally located, but not the quietest of
stablishments.

101

Morcote
Carina-Carlton, Via Cantonale, tel: 091 996 1131. Small
nd comfortable hotel.

iva del Garda
$$Sole, Piazza 3 Novembre 35, tel: 0464 552686. A ven-
able hotel; **$$Bellavista**, Piazza C Battisti 4, tel: 0464
54271; **$Bastione**, Via Bastione 19, tel: 0464 552652.
heap lodgings for gourmets.

Service with a smile

alò
$$Laurin, Viale Landi 9, tel: 0365 22022. Stylish art
ouveau hotel right next to the lake; **$$Benaco**, Lungo-
go Zanardelli 44, tel: 0365 20308. Modern hotel next
lake; **$Panoramica**, Via del Panorama 28, tel: 0365
1435. Appropriately-named, a short way outside town.

irmione
$$Villa Cortine Palace Hotel, Via Grotte 12, tel: 030
90 5890. Live like a prince in this luxury neoclassical
alazzo; **$$$Grand Hotel Terme**, Viale Marconi 7, tel:
30 916261. Five-star luxury, with its own thermal baths
d superb grounds; **$$$Sirmione**, Piazza Castello 19, tel:
30 916331. Very good service; **$$Golf et Suisse**, Via

Condominio 2, tel: 030 990 4590. Modern family hote
with its own beach; **$Benaco**, Via Colombare, tel: 03(
919103. A good place to see Sirmione and surrounding
on the cheap.

Stresa elegance

Stresa

$$$Des Iles Borromées, Lungolago Umberto I 31, tel
0323 938938. Elegant luxury hotel with much *grandezza*
in beautiful grounds; **$$Lido 'La Perla Nera'**, Viale Lid
Stresa 15, tel: 0323 33611, fax: 0323 933785. Nic
family-run establishment in a park.

Torbole

$$$Clubhotel La Vela, Via Strada Granda 2, tel: 046
505940. Popular with wealthy windsurfers; **$$Villa Verde**
Via Foci del Sarca 15, tel: 0464 505274. A quiet family
run establishment; **$Villa Clara**, Via Matteotti 13, tel
0464 505141. Cheap and comfortable.

Torri del Benaco

$$Gardesana, Piazza Calderini 20, tel: 045 722 5411. Tra
ditional hotel right next to the harbour, with an exceller
restaurant; **$Belvedere**, Via per Albisano, tel: 045 72
5088. Quiet and friendly.

Toscolano-Maderno

$$$Benaco, Lungolago Zanardelli 27, tel: 0365 2072<
Elegant and noble, in a magnificent park right next to th
lake; **$$Piccolo Paradiso**, Cecina-Messaga, tel: 036
643080. Cheap apartments, ideal for a family holiday
$Sole, Via Promontorio 7, tel: 0365 641335, simple hc
tel for those on a low budget.

Varese waiter

Varese

$$$Palace Hotel, Via Manara 11, tel: 0332 312600, fax
0332 31287. Comfortable and luxurious hotel in centra
position.

Verbania

$$$Majestic, Via Vittorio Veneto 32, tel: 0323 50430£
Luxury hotel with attractive grounds, right next to the lake
$$San Gotthardo, Piazza Imbarcadero 6, tel: 032
504465, good and reasonably-priced hotel.

Verona

$$$Due Torri Hotel Baglioni, Piazza S Ananstasia 4, te
045 595044. The most traditional five-star hotel in the city
$$Giulietta e Romeo, Via Tre Marchetti 3, tel: 045 8C
3554. Very comfortable, not only for lovers; **$Garda**, Vi
Gardesana 35, tel: 045 890 3877. Well situated betwee
the city and Lake Garda.

Index